Teaching

the Unteachable Student

50 Successful Strategies to Help Build Character
Amongst Challenging High School Youth

Nigel Francis

iUniverse, Inc.
Bloomington

iUniverse books may be ordered through booksellers or by contacting:

iUniverse
1663 Liberty Drive
Bloomington, IN 47403
www.iuniverse.com
1-800-Authors (1-800-288-4677)

Because of the dynamic nature of the Internet, any web addresses or links contained in this book may have changed since publication and may no longer be valid. The views expressed in this work are solely those of the author and do not necessarily reflect the views of the publisher, and the publisher hereby disclaims any responsibility for them.

Any people depicted in stock imagery provided by Thinkstock are models, and such images are being used for illustrative purposes only.

Certain stock imagery © Thinkstock.

ISBN: 978-1-4620-6749-7 (sc)
ISBN: 978-1-4620-6750-3 (e)

Printed in the United States of America

iUniverse rev. date: 4/10/2012

Dedication

This book is dedicated to my wife Kathleen who spent countless hours helping me with the editing process; to my two daughters (Nailah and Kailin) who have enriched my life greatly; to my mom and her husband Nick for their unending support; to my associate Kent Fanuzzi who has helped me to grow professionally; and to Dr. Fae Samuels who blessed me with an opportunity to teach. Finally, I dedicate this book to you the educator as you take on the challenge of educating our future leaders. Use this book to help students realize their full potential on their personal paths to success.

"A child educated in academics and not in character development has received only a partial education."

Nigel Francis

Contents

Preface

Teaching is an incredible vocation; one that I have been privileged to be a part of for close to a decade now. However, this profession offers both unique opportunities and distinct challenges. Educating young minds in the classroom is an enriching process, but the classroom is also a place where teachers must learn to deal with the ever-present obstacle of challenging behaviour. Teaching the Unteachable Student was written to help the classroom educator address and ultimately overcome challenging behaviours; this book offers strategies geared towards strengthening character development. In the context of this book, I define character (following Scanio in Character Education in the Classroom) as those traits or qualities that contribute to the way people act and behave in all areas of their lives.[1] In particular, there are six character traits, which I refer to as the "six key elements of character," that focus on improving the academic and behavioural performances of the most challenging students. They are:

- Respect,

- Responsibility,

- Perseverance,

---

1 Donna J. Scanio, *Character Education in the Classroom: Student Handbook* (Bloomington, Indiana: AuthorHouse, 2005), ix.

- Caring,

- Citizenship, and

- Trustworthiness.

Ultimately, each character trait must be developed for students to be successful in their social and academic endeavours. The strategies outlined in this book will enable teachers to help their students attain these markers of success. I refer to these strategies as the "Francis Rules." Each rule contains the following components:

1. The name of the individual rule or strategy.

2. One of the six key elements of character to be developed as a result of implementing the rule.

3. A detailed explanation of the use of the strategy and how to implement it.

4. The overall benefits of establishing this strategy for each of your students.

As you read this book, take the time to understand each of the individual Francis Rules. You will find that some rules will work better than others, depending on the student, so do not be afraid of trial and error. Keep your expectations high but do not assume that your students will embrace these rules overnight. Remember, character building is a process that requires time, commitment, and patience. As you commit to this approach, change will come. You will discover a new confidence in your abilities to manage your classes and to build stronger and more meaningful relationships with your students. Above all, have fun and remember that you can make a difference in the lives of your students.

For more information about this book or my other educational titles, please visit www.franciseduservices.ca. I wish you the best of luck during your school year. I am certain it will be an exciting journey as you set out to use these empowering strategies to assist you in *Teaching the Unteachable Student.*

Part 1

Dreams Versus Reality

Introduction

Do you remember where you were on January 20, 2009? If that date seems oddly familiar to you, it is because that was the day that Barack Obama became the forty-fourth president of the United States. I remember watching this spectacular moment unfold on the television at the high school where I teach. With the help of the school librarian, I brought my class down to the library to watch the historic event. The librarian eventually received so many requests from other teachers to bring their classes that it was decided that the big-screen television in the cafeteria would serve as a second location from which to view the inauguration. Both the library and the cafeteria were jam-packed as teachers and students watched this unprecedented moment together. It was truly a remarkable day to share with my colleagues and with students from all grade levels. I remember in the middle of the celebrations taking a moment to survey the students in the library. I noticed that on this day, teachers were not having to deal with challenging students. It was not as if these students were not in the room, because they were. There were simply no displays of attitude and thus no reprimands being given. These students (who on any other day would be classified as hard to teach) were in fact engaged in an uncommon but highly effective lesson. They were receptive to learning and exhibiting elements of strong character. The events that took place in the library affirmed for me two things that I already knew deep within my soul: The first is that with determination and patience, people can achieve great things ('Go, Obama, go!'). The second is that there is no such thing as an *unteachable* student.

The Dream

I have followed President Obama's rise to the White House from the moment he declared his candidacy in 2006. I have always been impressed with his ability to get things done despite the obstacles that lay before him. He and I share a very similar mindset – we are both not comfortable with the idea of giving up! I am hopeful that this notion holds true for you, the educator. If you think back to your days at teacher's college, you will probably remember the steady flow of individual reflections, long nights creating the perfect lessons, and countless articles that had to be read for the next day. However, during that extremely intense period of study, you always found a way to get things done despite the obstacles that stood before you. Failure was not an option, and this rationale was the foundation that you used to help you through your program. As a teacher-in-waiting, you had invested too much time, energy, and money to fail. You were determined to succeed.

All of that work brought us to one very special occasion – graduation. Take a moment to reflect on the events of that day. Personally, graduating from teacher's college gave me a real sense of accomplishment in my life. The feeling I had walking across the stage to receive my diploma, with my parents in the audience, justified all of the challenges that I endured. It was a day that had not come easily for me. In high school, I was never a straight-A student, and then I went to one community college and three different universities before obtaining my education certificate.

However, with the attitude that I was never going to give up, I eventually made it, and when I did, I was ecstatic. I was not just happy to be graduating because the course work had ended (although there was one class that I was glad to leave behind); I was equally happy for those individuals who would become my students in the future. I was excited at the opportunity to one day manage my own classroom and make a difference in students' lives. Equipped with ideas from leading educational thinkers, I had a strong desire to bring new teaching strategies into the classroom and create an academic environment in which all of my students could succeed. I made a promise to myself early in teacher's college that I would not fail them as their teacher and – equally important – I would not let them fail themselves as students. This is the dream I envisioned, but sadly, I have yet to achieve this reality for all of my students.

The Reality

Having graduated from teacher's college, I was lucky enough to secure a full-time teaching position, which I have now held for several years. My passion for teaching has only grown during this time, but I have become aware of some of the unique challenges that educators face when trying to create an environment "in which all students can succeed." Some of these challenges came from people and places that initially left me scratching my head in bewilderment. These sources included my relationships with parents, the school board, the administration, and even fellow faculty members. However, I would have to say that the most frustrating challenge that initially prevented me from guiding all of my students to achieve success was the students themselves. I found it hard to help them bring about their full potentials as students, not because they lacked the intelligence, but because they lacked the commitment and dedication that is needed to be successful within an academic institution. What I mean by this is that they were lacking in important qualities, such as persistence, respect, responsibility, and citizenship, to name a few. In essence, there were areas of their character that needed improvement. When I refer to *character*, I mean those traits or qualities that define "who we are [and that contribute to] the way we behave and act in all areas of our lives."[2] I am in no way suggesting that this was the sole reason for their lack of success in the classroom, but I believe that a weak foundation in character was certainly in part responsible.

Booker T. Washington once said that "Character is power." He was right in this declaration. Looking back through human history, we

---

2   Scanio, ix.

can find plenty of people who have used their strength of character to accomplish incredible feats. Some of these people include presidents like Abraham Lincoln, athletes like Terry Fox[3], and advocates like Rosa Parks. Most of my students reveal through their classroom practices that they understand that character is power. They come to class respecting themselves and others around them. They take their daily studies very seriously and rarely come up with excuses as to why they cannot succeed. However, there are those students in the class who do not act this way. These are the students whom I will refer to as "challenging." In my dealings with challenging students, I have observed that they can be selfish, lack persistence, and exhibit dishonesty. Rather than finding ways to succeed, these students find reasons for why they cannot. This attitude created a variety of classroom issues that I was forced to confront, which included truancy, disrespect for authority, inappropriate language and behaviour, and an overall lack of commitment to both education and personal growth. It was the reality that I faced. I must confess that initially, I was quite overwhelmed by these circumstances.

An unexpected internal battle began to emerge from within me. On the one hand, as a professional, I wanted to help these kids get an education and achieve their full potential as students, even if at times it brought me more stress than it did progress. However, personally I found it hard to want to help students who clearly indicated that they did not always want to help themselves. I was standing at a crossroads, and I was confused as to which direction I should take. A wise quote from the past helped me to get my bearings: "The ultimate measure of a [person] is not where he [or she] stands in moments of comfort and convenience, but

---

3   Terry Fox is a Canadian icon. In 1980, after losing his right leg to Cancer, he attempted to run across Canada in order to raise money for Cancer research.

where he [or she] stands at times of challenge and controversy." Whenever I've come to a crossroads in my life, these wise words of the late Martin Luther King Jr. always provide me comfort and guidance.

It has never been a part of my character to avoid a challenge, so I knew that whatever direction I took, I had to try to confront these issues. My first instinct was to seek advice from my colleagues. I remember going to see a teacher whom I highly respected. When I told him of my concerns about the lack of character some of my students were exhibiting, he jokingly pointed to his head and said, "Those kinds of kids are the reason why I am going bald." He kindly presented me with some sobering advice. It was his belief that some students exhibited weaker character than others and unless those individuals were willing to change, there was not much that could be done to alter their behaviour. In essence, he was saying that "you can lead a horse to water, but you can't make it drink." His advice came from his own personal battles as he had tried, on many occasions, to improve the individual characters of his challenging students. However, at the end of the day, he found that trying to improve their characters was time-consuming as well as frustrating. He felt this way because he did not get the necessary outside support to make any definitive changes with these students. He found that parents were often hard to reach, and even when he did manage to contact them, there was little to no change in the child's behaviour. Support from the school administration was equally deficient as the schools response to disobedience resulted in a system that created a revolving-door effect. A student would be sent to the office where he or she would receive a minor reprimand, and then that student would return to class the next day and display poor behaviour again, and so on. I thanked him for his time and his input, but to be frank, this was not the advice that I wanted to hear.

I decided to speak with a few more colleagues, but this time, I decided to change my approach. I brought up the issue in the staff room one day during lunch. It quickly became a hot topic with a variety of opinions being voiced. One teacher said, "Forget it – a bad seed is simply just that, a bad seed." Another teacher noted that, "Teachers can impact character, but as teachers, we only see students for an average of an hour a day. During the rest of the time, the students are being influenced by the media, music, and their peers. Therefore, what type of real change can occur during such a small window of opportunity?"

Another teacher noted that it was not her "job to teach character. This responsibility should fall in large part to the parents."

A final comment that I had taken from this discussion was for "teachers not to concern themselves with these students. Society (the 'real world') will deal with them once they leave high school." This was a lively debate, and it left me with plenty of food for thought.

I began to wonder if what my colleagues were saying had some genuine merit. I mean, even if teachers are equipped with sound classroom-management skills and the best of intentions, what kind of lasting impact could they have on their students' characters in just one semester? After I took some time to think further about the situation, it became clear to me that something could be done. I came to this conclusion in part for the following three reasons:

1. Character is not fixed.

2. Students desire success.

3. We must encourage students to avoid deviant behaviors.

Character Is Not Fixed

As I contemplated whether or not I could impact character in my classrooms, I came across a book entitled *The Power of Character.* In it, author Michael S. Josephson (the founder of Character Counts and the Josephson Institute of Ethics) states that in "no sense is anyone predestined to be good or bad, nor is a person's character permanently fixed ... ." I found that to be an interesting point of view, and it is one that I support. As human beings, we are not born simply with good or bad qualities; character is something that grows over time and can always be improved upon. Josephson also goes on to suggest that:

> Our human capacity to reason and choose makes the formation of our character an ongoing process. Each day we can decide to change our attitudes, re-evaluate and re-rank our values, and exercise a higher level of self-control to modify our behaviour. Yes, character is the cause of our actions, but it is also the result of our actions.[4]

As an adult and as a parent, I believe that my overall character is stronger now than it was when I was teenager. Some parts of my character evolved over time because of the people in my life and the lessons I learned. This is why I disagree with anyone who suggests that we, as teachers, cannot improve character. In fact, the very idea of improving character goes back to the very principles that we are required to uphold as teachers. We are bound to nurture and educate our students to become responsible citizens. To do this, we have to nourish both a student's intellectual ability (to help them to reason) and the development of their character (so that they can make good decisions). In other words, they need to be ready to go into society to be able to interpret laws; however,

4   Michael S. Josephson, ed., *The Power of Character*, 2nd ed. (Blooming-ton, Indiana: Unlimited Publishing, 1998), 3.

through their character, they must be able to make good decisions to follow laws and show compassion for others.

As educators, we are in a very unique position in that we have the power to be agents of change for our students every single day. I mean it seems obvious that if children are exhibiting low academic abilities in subject areas like Math, Science, and English, we as teachers can help them build those skills. We certainly do not expect them to come into class self-sufficient (if that were the case, society would not have much of a need for teachers.) Instead, we work with the skills that they have and build on them. We recognize that building their skills will be, as Josephson says, an "ongoing process." We do this even when the student is resistant and shows little interest in learning the particular topic or subject. So I ask you, is there any reason that the same could be not done for character? I think you will discover, as I did, that there is no reason at all.

Students Desire Success

A second reason that compelled me to tackle building character is that I have come to understand that all students want to be successful in life. I believe this to be true even if students are acting in a manner that will not produce success. I came to understand this point a few weeks into the fall semester of my second year of teaching. I was administering a lesson to a fairly new class. During the lesson, I asked my students who among them wanted to be successful. Of the twenty-seven students present, how many do you think raised their hands? The answer is every one of them. All twenty-seven students said that they wanted to be successful in their lives. In fact, if you were to ask any student in any classroom, you would be pretty hard pressed to find a student who would say, "No." It is no secret that to be successful in life, one needs to have strong character (and a little bit of luck). Since our students want success, we (as educators) would be doing them a disservice if we did not provide them with the necessary academic and character tools for them to achieve the success they desire. Some may suggest that challenging students lack ambition, but I do not find this to be the case. What we have are challenging students who have misguided values, and as educators, it is our job to try and reshape those values.

We Must Encourage Students To Avoid Deviant Behaviors.

A third and final reason that compelled me to want to tackle weak character had to do with a disturbing trend among teens occurring throughout North America. Former US Senator Pete Domenci writes in *The Power of Character* that "[t]here is an erosion of self discipline, self restraint and responsibility among our young people."[5] Lately, I have noticed that on any given day, you can pick up the newspaper and learn of a youth crime that has been committed. Headlines like "Youth Charged in Stabbing" or "Teen Faces Assault Charges" have become more a norm than a rarity. This disturbing trend really hit home for me when I read the local paper one day and discovered that one of the individuals charged in a weapons-related crime was a former student at my school.

The situation does not seem to be getting any better either; according to a 2008 study by Statistics Canada, violent and drug related crimes have increased steadiy since 1991.[6] As each day passes and we as teachers fail to take on the responsibility of building individual character, it creates a greater likelihood of a scenario where students go from committing minor delinquent acts in our classroom (such as skipping class) to committing major ones on our streets (such as murder). My colleague suggested that the "real world" would teach these kids a lesson, but I have come to realize that this is a lesson that we as a society cannot afford to have our students learning.

---

5   Josephson, 218.
6   Data from Statistics Canada 2008, Youth Crime Rates.

What adds to this problem is that as adolescent crime rates increase, we as a society spend too much time trying to the find the single source of the problem, when clearly there is no one definitive origin. In essence, we get caught up in the blame game. Everyone takes the time to point fingers at everyone else. Parents are pointing fingers at teachers; teachers are pointing fingers at the parents; and the politicians (ironically enough) point their fingers at the government. However, pointing fingers does little to solve the problem, because at the end of the day, the required value structure that these students need to be successful is still missing. This value structure will only become further out of reach if we as teachers choose not to do our part and take action for upcoming generations. This is why I have made a pledge to myself that students who come into my classroom with weak character traits will not be passed off to be somebody else's problem. I will do what I can in the time that we are together to improve the overall character of that individual, taking pride in even the smallest of advancements that he or she makes. Earlier, I mentioned that one of my colleagues had quoted the proverb "You can lead a horse to water, but you can't make it drink." This is true for the most part –you can't force a horse to drink water; however, you certainly can encourage that horse to want to quench its thirst. If we want to help produce strong and law-abiding citizens in the high school system, teachers need to strategize and remain cognizant not only of our needs but those of our students' needs as well. We can do this by understanding what is relevant in their lives, and how they see and experience the world. Remaining aware of these factors in the classroom requires hard work. We cannot afford to be impatient with students; rather, we must demonstrate a high a degree of patience and understanding. We will never know what progress can be made until we decide to put our best foot forward every day for every student.

Tools for the Job

As I committed myself to character building in the classroom, I began to develop a series of strategies. These strategies not only worked well in my classroom, but my colleagues also had great success using them with their challenging students. It is because of my personal success and their feedback that I have decided to share these strategies with you. *Teaching the Unteachable Student* is a practical, educational resource that will enable educators to help their students establish a strong foundation in character. These strategies focus on building up what I refer to as the "six key elements of character," which I mentioned at the beginning of this book. These six key elements are: Respect, Responsibility, Perseverance, Caring, Citizenship, and Trustworthiness. Developing these six key elements of character will increase the success that challenging students can achieve during and beyond high school. As an educator, I am confident that these strategies will make a difference in your classroom and increase the level of optimism for both you and your students. It is time for a new beginning; it is time to *Teach the Unteachable Student.*

Part 2

*A New Beginning
Strategies 1 through 25*

Francis Rule #1: Building Character Is a Requirement Not an Option

Character-Building Component: All Six Elements of Character

"To educate a person in mind and not in morals is to educate a menace to society." Despite the age of former American president Theodore Roosevelt's declaration, the premise of this statement continues to resonate in the 21st century. Some might argue that teachers are primarily responsible for educating a child's mind while the parents should be responsible for educating their child in morals. Although I understand the reasoning behind this type of thinking, this is an opinion with which I respectfully disagree. Teachers need to teach students their ABC's (there is no questioning this), but they also must be responsible for teaching students right from wrong. Students can spend anywhere from six to eight hours a day at their respective secondary schools. When you add on top of that time for homework and after-school activities, this does not leave parents with much opportunity during the week to teach and reinforce positive values.

As children enter their formative teenage years, teaching values must not be considered to be something that occurs predominately within the home; rather, it is important to recognize that learning takes place continually throughout the day, which means children are developing their value set at school.

It is critical that students continue to learn values outside of the home, because whatever positive values were taught to children as they were growing up will be tested daily as they make their transition into high school. As a high school teacher, I am sure that you are well aware that it is a place where peer pressure is in full bloom. It knows no boundaries and impacts almost every student. In the book *Surviving Peer Pressure for Teens,* the authors Hilary Cherniss and Jane Sluke appropriately refer to the teenage years as the "Peer Pressure Squeeze." They go on to say that "Peer Pressure is a major force in the life of every teenager [as] it causes anxiety strong enough to shake even the strongest wills."[7] A student may come to high school with a strong foundation in character, but this can be easily eroded as students look to be accepted by and fit in with their peers.

Every year, I witness this transformation with the freshman class at my school. Some of these students remind me of Wally and Beaver Cleaver from the 1960s hit TV show *Leave It to Beaver.* They come to high school with a flawless appearance and attitude. They are dressed for success, organized and courteous, and have all the supplies they need. However, by midsemester, there is definitely a shift in attitude. In an effort to win popularity and expand their circle of friends, the once-flawless appearance will change –and not for the better. These kids are no longer the Cleavers but rather they look and sound like the mischievous and scheming Eddie Haskel (Eddie was friends with the Cleaver boys, and he was always up to no good). They seem to adopt a new value set that includes behaviours like skipping class, not handing in assignments, using abusive language, and inhaling and ingesting a variety of harmful substances. They are indifferent about lying and get involved in sexual relations during stages of development in which they cannot make sound judgements; these decisions lead to premature parenthood for some. As these students look to be accepted, their values are slowly picked at and modified to match those of their newfound friends. These values can be very dangerous ones to

---

7   Hilary Cherniss and Jane Sluke. The Complete Idiots Guide to Surviving Peer Pressure for Teens. New York: Alpha Books, 2001, xii.

take on, as they are usually affiliated with popular culture and the mainstream media. Money, violence, fashion, and breaking the rules are considered to be cool. Education, working hard, and following the rules are, unfortunately, not. As our students spend so much of their time in an environment like this, parents cannot be expected to navigate their children through these treacherous obstacles alone. Teachers must also take on this responsibility to combat false values. We must help to curb bad behaviour and promote positive character in our students.

In high school, building character should be regarded by teachers as a requirement and not an option. We as teachers must pick up where the parent has left off or, in some cases, add what the parents have failed to teach. If you are like me, you may not like the idea of taking on additional responsibilities that increase your already overloaded work schedule. However, the task of building character need not be regarded as another arduous duty. Character education is not a separate subject matter that has to be incorporated into your daily teachings. Character education is one of those branches of learning that is already part of your daily educational curriculum. Since it already exists, there is no new subject for us to create. All we have to do is highlight those individual character traits that we want our students to value.

For example, if you are a Science teacher tutoring students on Albert Einstein's theory of relativity, you could take a few minutes to talk about Einstein the man. You could ask your students what elements of character Einstein possessed that allowed him to present such a complicated idea. Or if you were studying Law, you might stress in your lesson why telling the truth is so important in our society. Point out to students individuals who have been caught lying (like Bill Clinton, who lied under oath) and let them see for themselves the kind of harm that lying can create. Making these simple connections is not overly time-consuming for you but helps your students immeasurably by keeping character education at the forefront of their minds. As teachers, we must view building character as a shared responsibility between those individuals who care for the students in the home and those of us who care for the students in our schools.

Building Character behind the Scenes:

As your course progresses and you continually stress the importance of building character, your students will eventually come to take building their own character more seriously. This will help to counteract the false values that our students are bombarded with on a daily basis.

Francis Rule #2: Remember, Rome Was Not Built in a Day

Character-Building Component: All Six Elements of Character

Building a genuine relationship is never easy. I was reminded of this when I first met my wife. When we met, we were not exactly the "perfect match." She had been born and raised in the country, and I grew up in the city; she lived in the moment, while I planned for the future. We seemed to be at odds in many areas of our lives, but what makes us so compatible (and eventually led us down the aisle) is our ability to accept one another for who we are (not to mention that she has a great smile). In education, the teacher-student relationship can also be considered a far-from-perfect match. Although teachers strive to create and maintain positive relationships with their students, it can be tricky, because of their differing attitudes. Teachers want challenging students to adjust their behaviour and conform to a mentality that puts education first; meanwhile, students may often demonstrate attitudes that show little regard for following rules and for the value of education. While this dynamic is not ideal for a long-lasting relationship, it is the daily reality that teachers experience. A central question that emerges is: where do educators go from here?

The answer can be found by applying two key steps. The first is to accept students for who they are regardless of their inadequacies or attitudes towards education. The second step is to realize that no relationship can be built without trust, and building this trust takes time. In my classes, there are no preconditions for students to receive my tutelage or kindness. When students are exhibiting poor character in my classroom, I remind myself that these habits did not manifest themselves overnight. Their poor behaviour will not be reversed with one or two impassioned lectures, delivered by me, that end up with ultimatums and immediate timelines for improvement. Instead, I work towards building a rapport with the students first. As an educator, it is critical that students view you as a person who has insight into their developing identities and the hardships they face on their journey to adulthood. They need to know that you are not evaluating them based on past mistakes but on their current performance and behaviour. In no way am I suggesting that you should not address and modify inappropriate behaviours. However, this is a process that needs to develop gradually. Just as Rome was not built in a day, developing a positive relationship with challenging students takes time, acceptance, and patience.

Applying these two key steps – accepting students for who they are and allowing time for trust to develop – will help you immensely in establishing genuine relationships with your students. From here, take pride in even the smallest of gains that you make to improve your students' character and continue to build upon them.

Building Character behind the Scenes:

As you go through the process of building a relationship based on acceptance, trust, and patience with your students, you open the door to multiple improvements in their character. Love your students for who they are, and help guide them to become their best selves.

Francis Rule #3: Education Comes First, Even in Times of Conflict

Character-Building Component: Responsibility

Can you recall a situation in which friends or family members have gotten into an argument and refused to speak to one another? How long did this dispute last? Was it a week, a year, or maybe the situation is still unresolved? In high schools across North America, this type of scenario occurs daily, and the arguments are not just between students. Students and teachers can also find themselves embroiled in disagreements. When this happens, the parties may not see eye to eye with one another and may become entrenched in their positions. The teachers are looking for the students to be punished for their actions, while the students believe that their behaviour was justified and do not see the point in the consequences. The impasse begins, and the students are sent to the office. However, if the conflict is not resolved quickly, it is the students who pay the ultimate price, as they are no longer in the classroom learning. So the question then becomes: what can be done to minimize any potential loss to the student's education?

If you find yourself involved in a dispute with a student and you see no other option than for them to be sent to the office, the following steps should be taken to ensure that their education is not compromised in any way:

1. **Provide Students With Work to Complete While They Wait in the Office.**

When my students and I find ourselves involved in an argument that I feel cannot be settled in class, I may send them to the office. Although this solution stops the disruption in my classroom, these students have the potential of losing out on valuable class time if an administrator cannot see them right away (for example, if an administrator is busy dealing with other school-related incidents or is not available to see the student until the following day). In the interim, the student is left with little to do while he or she waits. This is a scenario that I consider to be problematic, because every minute that a challenging student spends in the office and not in the classroom learning can potentially put him or her further behind in the course. My goal in sending that student out of the classroom is to have the inappropriate behaviour addressed; it is never my intention to put the student's education on hold. This is why I find it useful to send down classroom work with the students who find themselves in the office for an extended period of time. This is a simple but helpful strategy that requires students to complete their work and be responsible for their education even in times of conflict.

2. **Students Need to Return to the Classroom as Quickly as Possible.**

When I have gotten involved in conflicts with challenging students and have sent them to the office, I cannot honestly say that I have always been in a rush to have them return to my class. However, despite my personal feelings, returning to the classroom is in their best interest. This is easier said than done. There have been times when I have been so upset with a student that, for my own sanity, I would recommend to the administrator that the student stay in the office. That being said, the office environment can never compare to a classroom in terms of what a student can learn. As teachers, we must always remember that education comes first. After a conflict, we must not allow our personal feelings to impact a student's quick transition back into the classroom. I am not suggesting that the student's actions do not warrant being sent out; but rather, it is our responsibility as educators to always act in the student's best interest. This means in times of conflict returning students to the classroom as quickly as possible so that they are able resume their full educational experience. Although this is not an easy strategy to implement, it is one that must be used. It will help to keep challenging students on track and will enable them to be responsible for their education.

Building Character behind the Scenes:

As educators, we know from experience that despite any problems or conflicts occurring in our lives, we still have a responsibility to get our jobs done. Students need to be held to the same standard and learn this lesson sooner rather than later.

Francis Rule #4: Organization, Organization, Organization

Character-Building Component: Responsibility

If you have challenging students in your classroom, then chances are they are lacking in organizational skills. This can directly affect whether or not they bring the appropriate school supplies to class (e.g., writing utensils) and whether or not they manage to hand in their assignments on time, or at all. This is problematic because if this type of scenario occurs throughout the semester, students run the risk of falling behind. As students see their chances for success diminishing, they may become discouraged and essentially give up on the course. A simple and effective solution to try to change this situation is not to request a new student (if only it were that easy); but rather, to get students to improve their organizational skills. The following are two suggestions on how you might go about doing this.

1. Supplies

When students do not bring the proper writing utensils to class, it can make for a difficult time for both students and teachers. For students, this means that they do not have the proper tools to take notes, thus decreasing their chances of retention. Meanwhile, for teachers, this can create a situation in which they either need to supply writing utensils, or if unable, allow the student to just sit in the class doing nothing. We all know what happens next: the student gets bored and begins to chitchat and the teacher may have to deal with disciplinary issues. Often, when students do not bring any writing utensils, it is because they do not return the utensils to any one set place. Sometimes the pen or pencil goes behind their ears; other times they may place it in their pockets or even at the bottom of their bags. A good strategy to change this is to get students in the habit of placing their writing utensils in the same place consistently. Ideally, this should be in some pocket of their napsack or in a pencil case. This will help students to keep track of their writing utensils.

2. Missed Assignments

Challenging students can easily lose track of when assignments are due. As a result, they often need extra time to hand in the assignment late, or if too much time passes, they end up not handing it in at all. To avoid this, a day planner would be an excellent educational tool to help them keep track of their assignments and weekly responsibilities. I have noticed that those students who do well in my courses usually bring a day planner to class. In fact, as a teacher, I could not imagine trying to track my daily responsibilities without one. This is why I make it a high priority that all of my students have an agenda within three days of coming to my class. This is not a difficult request to comply with, as most school boards provide students with agendas at the beginning of the year.

Expect to find that some of your challenging students may be resistant to the idea of using an organizer. They may even come up with some pretty creative reasons as to why this is the case (my favourite is that they don't need to write things down because they can keep track of what they have to do in their heads). If this is the case, I remind them of their current grade and simply ask them to give this a shot to see if things can improve. The best scenario is that they try it, and the worst is that they do not. One of the best comments that I heard from one of my challenging students who decided to take me up on my offer was that she "never knew being organized could be this easy."

If challenging students are able to bring their writing utensils to class consistently and keep track of when assignments are due, they will soon realize that academic success does not come by chance; it comes, in part, with organization.

Building Character behind the Scenes:

As students begin to organize themselves, their motivation to meet their daily responsibilities will increase, and they will consistently arrive with the writing utensils to get the job done.

Francis Rule #5: Avoid Yelling When Reprimanding a Student

Character-Building Component: Respect

In teacher's college, it was emphasized by my professors that a quality of a good teacher was to make one's presence known in one's classroom. This was important to help teachers maintain control and discourage students from misbehaving. During some of my student teaching placements, I saw examples of classrooms in which the teachers had little control over their students' conduct because they were quite hesitant to reprimand and discipline. I was determined that this was not going to happen to me. As I was known for having a loud voice, I wanted to use this to my advantage. I figured the louder my voice, the larger my presence would be. As a first-year teacher, it was my intention to get my students to think twice before they acted inappropriately, because they knew Mr. Francis would not be afraid to raise his voice and reprimand them. Right from the start, I had some success using this approach. Whether I was asking students to stop talking during a lesson or to put their cell phones away and get back to work, they knew that I was serious by the pitch in my voice.

As the years passed and I began to focus my attention on building character in my classrooms, I started to question if raising my voice was the most effective way to get students to follow my instructions. I questioned this in large part for two reasons:

The first was the way I felt during and after the conflict. Sometimes I would feel extremely juvenile, having been involved in a shouting match with an adolescent. I also became concerned about my overall mood. I found it hard to let go of the frustration I was feeling, and this would affect my mood for the rest of the day.

Secondly, I began to wonder what underlying message the students were receiving, watching me respond to conflict in this way. As a veteran teacher, I know that students model what they see. I became concerned that perhaps they were interpreting from my actions that you need only raise your voice to get people to do what you want. If this was the case, I knew that this was not the message I wanted to send.

As a result of my experience, I recommend as a strategy that teachers avoid yelling when reprimanding a student. It is important that when students act inappropriately we let them know their behaviour is causing a disruption; however, we must do this in a way that preserves our integrity and does not let us lose control of our emotions. Yelling can quickly lead to losing control of the situation and acting in a manner that is not in line with our character. I find that if students are truly intent on defying my wishes, then raising my voice at them will only help to inflame the situation. If we want our students' overall character to be strengthened, we should strive for them to act appropriately not because they fear their teachers but because it is the right thing to do.

Building Character behind the Scenes:

Raising your voice to reprimand a student is usually inappropriate and disrespectful. As you begin the process of moving away from yelling at your students, you will find that you are providing an excellent model for students of how they should respond in moments of conflict.

Francis Rule #6: Emphasize Etiquette, If You Please

Character-Building Component: Citizenship

At the start of my classes, I always take a moment to greet my students by saying hello. One would hope that such a polite gesture would be reciprocated by all in the room, but this is not always the case. Should I find that this polite gesture has gone unreturned, I take no offence. I simply make a point to repeat myself until all of my students have acknowledged and reciprocated my greetings. I can either do this by speaking to the entire class or by speaking directly to those students who failed to respond. Call me old school, but I adhere to the idea that "manners maketh [the person]."[8] I want students to embody this idea as well. You may find that some of your students shy away from using basic etiquette skills. Getting them to use phrases like "Good morning," "Please," or "Excuse me" on their own may be quite difficult. Some students believe that etiquette is a matter of choice (they don't have to do it if they don't feel like it); this mind-set is one that I find to be unacceptable. We must reinforce to students that etiquette is not an optional feature like you would add or decline on a new car. It is an essential component to being a good citizen and must be practiced at all times. Some of the things we can do in our classes to promote etiquette are the following:

1. When students answer questions in class, make sure that you always thank them for their comments.

2. Do not allow students to ask for supplies from anyone without saying "Please" and "Thank you."

---

8   William of Wykeham (1324–1404).

3. At the beginning and ending of any class, acknowledge your students by saying "Hello" and "Good-bye." As they are getting ready to leave, thank them for coming to class and express your hope that they enjoy the rest of the day.

4. If you are in the process of speaking with a student, make sure that other students who may want your attention do not interrupt without a polite interjection (e.g., "Excuse me," "Pardon me," and so forth). If this occurs, let them know that you are busy at the moment, but add (to reassure them) that you will get back to them once you have concluded the current conversation.

5. Often, I make a point that whenever my students and I leave the classroom, either to go on a school trip or to the library, I always ask the young gentlemen in my class to hold the doors open for the young ladies on our way to any destination. On the way back, I have the ladies return the favour or vice versa.

6. Sometimes when students ask for clarification, they may be inclined to say, "Huh?" or "What?" Make a point to have them repeat themselves and say, "Pardon?" or "Excuse me?"

These are simple suggestions to follow. They require little effort on your part, but they send a big message to your students that you value etiquette.

Building Character behind the Scenes:

If we did not treat one another with basic etiquette, our society would suffer as a result. Through your efforts, students will come to understand that etiquette is a key component to being a good citizen. When we continue to demand that our students practice and demonstrate basic etiquette, we will be that much further ahead in making our society more civil.

Francis Rule #7: Keep in Mind that Not All Students Are Raised in the Same Way

Character-Building Component: All Six Elements of Character

Every child is raised differently. I remember this point as I watch my eldest daughter grow. When my wife and I found out that she was pregnant, we were committed from day one to bringing up our daughter in a nurturing and caring environment. Even before she was born, my wife and I were involved in the parenting process. We made sure that my wife was eating healthy foods and vitamins. On top of that, we even talked and read to our daughter and played classical music for her while she was in the womb. These were some of the initial steps we took as parents to raise our daughter. As a result of our commitment, our daughter is developing into a kind, generous, and respectful human being. My wife and I spend countless hours reinforcing positive values so that by the time our daughter reaches high school, she will have a foundation in character that makes her strong, respectful, and a person who puts education first. I do not mention how my wife and I parent to suggest that our parenting style is flawless, because that is far from the case. Rather, I want to illustrate that right or wrong, all parents will bring up their children the way that they feel is best. Parents will raise their children in part based on their education, cultural values, and the resources available to them. To some degree, this will have an impact on a child's overall character.

Understandably, I often see a high level of frustration amongst teachers when they have to teach challenging students. One of their concerns is that they are annoyed by having to spend time teaching values that they believe the student should have learned in the home. As a strategy to building character, we must keep in mind that our students are not carbon copies. Each has been raised differently, and, as mentioned earlier, this will have an impact on their overall character. As some students may display weaker character than others, it is necessary that teachers exude patience and understanding to help those students further develop personally and academically. As teachers, we cannot control the types of students who come into our classrooms. However, what we can control is what the students learn while they are in our company. This means reshaping the values of those students whom we find challenging to teach. That being said, it is important that you be realistic with your goals. Often, if we try to transform our students' characters completely, our efforts may be met with disappointment. Instead, try to improve just one element of character at a time and continuously try to build upon this.

Building Character behind the Scenes:

As teachers, if we can begin to care for our challenging students despite their shortcomings, then these students may begin to care more about helping themselves. This is a necessary starting point for individual success.

Francis Rule #8: Talk with Parent(s)/Guardian(s)

Character-Building Component: Responsibility

As you set out to build character in your classroom, I would suggest that you not embark on this journey alone. Caregivers are key allies and must be involved in the character-building process with your students. I have helped my fair share of students re-evaluate and rebuild aspects of their character; however, this task would have been much more difficult without the individual support of a caregiver. A perfect example of this arose with a student whom I will refer to as Chris.

In my third year of teaching, Chris showed up to my class as a young man ready for success. He was polite and eager to learn, and I will never forget his brilliant smile. However, by midsemester, I noticed a complete 180-degree turn in Chris' behaviour. He began to arrive to class late; he was no longer handing in all of his assignments; and that once brilliant smile was rarely visible. Chris no longer acted like a young man who was ready to be successful. Unfortunately, his character was changing right before my eyes.

Initially, I thought that because Chris had shown so much promise at the beginning of the course, a quick pep talk might do the trick to get him back on track. However, it quickly became apparent that this young man needed a more substantial intervention. I say this because I discovered that Chris had taken up company with some very immature and irresponsible schoolmates. He was being strongly influenced by his peers, and these new friends did not have his best interests at heart. Chris was in no position to change things around, but I knew something had to be done. I decided to call home to see if Chris' mom would be able to assist in this situation. I called home a few times during the day, but unfortunately, each time I did, I was greeted by voice mail. My next step was to try to reach Chris' mom after school. Thankfully, I was able to reach her but not until very late in the evening. I would learn from this conversation that she worked ten- to twelve-hour shifts five days a week. When I first told Chris' mother of my concern, she was understandably upset.

It was hard for her to accept this type of news. She informed me that as a single parent, she had worked very hard and had not raised Chris to act in this manner. She told me that if her son was indeed acting this way, she had no intention of putting up with it. She asked if she could come to school and meet with me to see Chris' behaviour firsthand. Initially, I was a little uneasy with the idea. I mean, having a parent come to the school to watch her child's behaviour seemed like a scene from a movie. However, this was not a movie, and after some careful consideration, I decided that this could benefit Chris.

A few days later, Chris' mother came to the school. She came directly to my classroom, and from there, we proceeded to the second-floor window. At this location, she had a clear view of her son and his behaviour as he hung out with his friends during lunch in the forum.

As I said earlier, this was no Hollywood movie, but if I were a screenwriter, I could not have written a better script. Chris was wearing his uniform in a manner that his mom was not accustomed to seeing. His pants were hung well below his waist, almost around his thighs. In fact, they were so low you could see the designer label that had been sewn onto his underwear. Also, he was wearing his baseball cap inside the school, which was clearly against school policy. A passing teacher stopped and asked Chris to take it off. He complied, but the minute the teacher turned the corner, he put the hat right back on. To top it off, Chris had his MP3 player on display. He was also not permitted to have such devices out during the school day; it should have been in his locker. The look on Chris' mother's face reflected true confusion and shock. She could not believe that she was looking at her son. It took some pretty swift talking on my part to stop her from going down to the forum to confront him on the spot. That type of confrontation might have created a whole different scenario than the one I envisioned.

I reminded Chris' mom that her son's performance outside of the classroom was only half of what she needed to see. His performance inside the classroom also required observation. When lunch was over, Chris' mom went into my class and took a seat at the back of the room. It would be here that his mom would confront her son. Chris was almost fifteen minutes late. When he arrived, he brought with him a stellar excuse for his tardiness. He told me that his locker was stuck, and he'd had a hard time getting it open. His uniform was still messy and disorganized. I normally request that all of my students get into proper uniform before they enter my class, but on this day, I thought I would let it slide. Chris did not notice his mother until he was about halfway down to his seat. I could see him do a quick double take. The look on his face was, as they say, "priceless" as he slowly sat down. It was a combination of both horror and disbelief. I never let on to the other students that Chris' mother was in the class, but he sure knew. The icing on the cake was when I asked Chris to take out his homework from the night before. He did not have it with him. He tried to give an excuse as to why it was not here, but his mom was in no mood to hear excuses. His mother gave him a look I can still remember. I can happily say that Chris changed his behaviour – and quickly. For the rest of the semester, Chris' mother and I spoke once every two weeks. Chris knew that he would have to answer to his mother if she did not get a glowing report. I am pleased to say that I never had another problem with this young man for the rest of the semester.

This interaction between a teacher and a caregiver was quite a successful one. However, I know that this type of positive outcome does not always occur. As an educator, you may have had some negative experiences dealing with parents. If that is the case, do not let those encounters discourage you from interacting with other parents. The following strategies and considerations may help you in your future dealings with parents:

Call home to give both positive and negative feedback.

No caregiver looks forward to speaking with a teacher who calls only when he or she has something negative to say about the child. This is why it is important to build a relationship of communication that is based on praise as well as concern. Be sure to call the house to let caregivers know when their child has done something wrong, but equally important, you need to call the house to inform caregivers when their child has done something right. When you do this, caregivers will be able to view you objectively. This ultimately will allow them to see you as a teacher who has their child's best interests at heart.

Try calling after school hours.

Not all students have parents at home from nine to five. I have seen teachers make phone calls during the day and become frustrated when they do not reach anyone at home. If you are having trouble reaching parents during the day, you may want to contact them after hours in the evening. This may cut into your personal time, but it will increase your chances of speaking to a parent.

Your immediate concerns may not be those of the caregiver.

Often when we call a parent about a problem that has occurred at school, we want parents to devote their full attention to the matter. Unfortunately, this is not always the case. Try to remember that caregivers have a variety of challenges to face throughout their day and may not see your particular concerns as their top priority. This may not sound very practical, but it is a reality. Should you call a parent and meet with resistance or get an inadequate response to your concern, do not become discouraged. When working with a caregiver to help a child build character, we should not be looking for immediate results; instead, we ought to look at things as a work in progress. Parents may need more time to clear their own agendas so that they can devote time to addressing your concerns.

If you are unable to reach a parent on the phone, send a letter.

If you have tried calling a caregiver and you have been unable to reach him or her, try sending a letter. It is important that you do not give up trying to contact the caregivers, as this communication is crucial to the well-being of your students.

Follow Up

When you have called to speak to caregivers regarding concerns you have, make sure that you follow up and give them a report about what events have taken place since your conversation. If you are successful at keeping a continuous dialogue between you and the caregivers, this will increase the chance that the student's behaviour will improve.

Building Character behind the Scenes:

If students feel that both their parents and their teachers are concerned about their welfare, this can help to increase their chances of making themselves accountable for their actions both at school and at home.

Francis Rule #9: Hurry Up with that Marking

Character-Building Component: Responsibility

When I signed on to be a teacher, I never realized how much of my time would be occupied marking assignments. Whether it is during your spare time throughout the day, at home in the evening, or even at the family cottage on the weekends, there is always something that needs to be marked. With such a tremendous workload, it can be quite the struggle to hand back assignments *on time*, but believe me when I say that as a strategy, it is in your students' best interests to do exactly that. Below are three key reasons why handing back assignments must be a high priority:

1. **You get to know sooner rather than later who has handed in assignments and who is avoiding responsibility.**

Initially, whenever I assigned a due date for assignments, I would collect them at the end of the period. I usually just asked students to place their assignments on my desk. The problem with this method was that it never became immediately clear to me who handed in their assignment on time. I would only learn about those individuals who had failed to hand in the assignment after I had marked them all. To avoid this problem, I changed my approach. Now when students come up to my desk, I call them up one at a time and check off their names as they hand in their work. Using this method provides an opportunity to speak with students immediately if they failed to hand in the assignment. As students realize that they will be held accountable for not handing in their work (on the day the assignment is due), this helps to motivate them to hand in their work on time so they will not have to deal with any potential consequences.

2. **It is hard to climb a mountain.**

I am sure you have witnessed that when some of your challenging students fall behind in their work, they can become very discouraged. They can throw in the towel too quickly believing that it is impossible for them to get back on track with their assignments. The fallout of this can be disastrous as students may come to class less frequently, leading to even more missed assignments. Marking papers as soon as possible gives you the opportunity not only to identify and help those students who have not handed in assignments, but to help eliminate the possibility of multiple assignments piling up and not getting completed.

3. **Marks are a great motivator.**

When you hand back work quickly, your students will receive timely feedback that lets them know where they stand in your class. Believe me when I say that they look forward to reading your comments. There have been times when I have been far behind in my marking, with anywhere from two to four assignments that needed to be marked. If I had a student who failed to hand in three of the four assignments, this student would be in serious jeopardy of not passing my class. Though there is no doubt that the fault lay with the student for not handing in the assignment, I did not give the student my best effort by marking the assignments earlier and detecting his or her omissions. If students are continuously reminded about where they stand in your course (as opposed to just at midterm), this can help to motivate them to keep up with their work.

Building Character behind the Scenes:

As you mark assignments in a timely manner, this will help to keep students on track and responsible for handing in their work.

Francis Rule #10: Focus on Education and Character Development When Disciplining Students

Character-Building Component: Citizenship

As a new teacher, it is always a good idea to look to your colleagues for guidance and mentorship. When I began working in education, there were many individuals who helped to guide and mentor me, but the one person who stands out is my former principal. For purposes of privacy, I will refer to her as Principal Kelly. Principal Kelly had a very unique style when it came to dealing with any students who challenged school authority and needed disciplinary action. Principal Kelly, in a calm tone and demeanour, reminded the student that at our school, students were there for two primary reasons. The first was education, and the second was learning. She regarded education as a gift, and she let the student know that it was not to be wasted. She would often follow up by suggesting that if the student had any concern with her policies, he or she had the option to transfer to a school that offered something different. There would rarely be a need for further discussion or consequences, but if further discipline was required, Principal Kelly made a point to focus her discipline around education and character development. In other words, she never disciplined just to punish a student; rather, she disciplined to remind students that education comes first. What I admired about this approach was that as she disciplined, she made the students think about how their actions were harming their education. It was these types of encounters that led the students to respect, listen to, and trust Principal Kelly. She was an inspirational individual, and I knew her approach was one that I needed to follow.

As I watched Principal Kelly incorporate education into her disciplinary approach, I knew that this was a strategy that could help me in the classroom. This was when I really began to stress to students that the main goal of education was not receiving A's or B's; rather, education was about personal empowerment. This philosophy allowed students to be in charge of their own destinies. Finally, I let students know that I would not let anything get in the way of them receiving their education. This message was evident in virtually every aspect of my classroom, including my course outline, lesson planning; and the décor of my room, and like my principal, it was a key tool that I used in disciplining my students. Some of my discipline methods included:

- Essays – One that I find resonates well is to have students write a paper explaining how their inappropriate actions today have helped them to further their educational career.

- Biography Reports – having students write a report on key individuals who have obtained great success throughout their lives and how education played a role in those people's success.

- Detentions – students must come to my detentions and write a paper that outlines why their actions were inappropriate and in what ways they dishonoured their family name.

Students quickly understood that these disciplines were not about punishment; rather, they revealed my concern for their well-being and personal growth. As teachers, when we decide to discipline, we should ensure that our consequences help students to reflect on their actions and force them to think about the person that they are today and the person that they want to become in the future.

Building Character behind the Scenes:

When you consistently focus your classroom around education, learning, and building character, students will begin to see the relevance in these methods. They will become better citizens as a result and will be more likely to respect your rules in the classroom.

Francis Rule #11: If It Is Working, Don't Quit

Character-Building Component: All Six Elements of Character

The beginning of the school year is an exciting time for teachers. Many have taken the opportunity to think "outside of the box" and develop new activities that promote learning and engagement. New activities are always fun to create and implement, but the downside to them is the amount of time and energy that must be invested to make them work. A perfect example of this is what happened to a former colleague of mine who had a great idea. She had decided that she was going to make an interactive website for her class. On the website, students could look up their marks, download class handouts, see important dates, and even chat online about course-related topics. This was an ambitious project, but it would be beneficial. The problem for her was that the project was taking up a lot of her personal time. As a result, my colleague did not know whether to keep the website going or to close it down altogether.

My advice for my colleague was not to end the project. Rather, I suggested that she scale back on some of her intentions. Rather than uploading grades for every assignment, she could just upload student standings at the end of each unit. I also told her that she did not have to take on this task alone. Her school's tech department should have some savvy senior students who could help her to maintain the website. As far as working from home, I told her that she should limit the amount of time there. She should instead set some regular hours or days when she either came into school early in the morning or stayed later to get the work done.

The bottom line was that since the class was responding in a favourable manner to the website, there was no way she could just stop it entirely. Yes, it was taking up some of her time, but the end result was that her students were engaged.

As a strategy, should you find yourself in a similar position, do not even think of throwing in the towel just because you are finding the project to be a little time-consuming. Every project initially takes a lot of energy to start, but I find that once it is up and running, it becomes easier and easier to maintain. Should you find yourself overwhelmed, don't be afraid to ask for help or modify your initiative. Helping your students to build their character and improve their overall academic performance is well worth the effort.

Building Character behind the Scenes:

Your ability to design creative classroom activities has the potential to impact all six elements of your students' characters.

Francis Rule #12: Include a Character Education Component in Your Lesson Plans

Character-Building Component: All Six Elements of Character

Have you ever delivered a great lesson? Do you remember that euphoric feeling you had as you looked out at your students during the period? This is a great moment for any teacher because you can see on your students' faces that they understand the message you are delivering. Rarely does this type of moment happen by chance; more often than not, moments like these occur because you were prepared. More than likely, you put together a strong lesson plan that outlined your objectives, included interactive activities, and balanced the subject matter over the duration of the class. In essence, the message that you wanted your students to grasp was developed well in advance. I suggest using the same type of approach when trying to teach character. In the same way that you created a lesson plan to deliver your subject matter, as a strategy, you should create a lesson plan that includes a character education component. When you take this approach, you can focus ahead of time on the core values that you want your students to learn and on what days you want to teach these values. This provides a variety of benefits for both you and your students. These include: measuring comprehension, time management, and balancing values.

Measuring Comprehension

Most schools provide, within their curricula, the opportunity to teach values. However, these values are usually taught implicitly as opposed to explicitly. The problem with teaching values implicitly is that it is hard to determine whether the student has grasped the intended value. By incorporating a character education component into your lessons, you create an opportunity to discuss specific values openly. Furthermore, you can confirm and measure that your students understand these values using evaluation tools, such as unit assessments, class discussions, and verbal or written responses.

Time Management

Another area of concern when you teach character implicitly is that the time spent on each value can be inconsistent and vary substantially. When you create a lesson plan that designates specific character traits to be learned, you can more clearly establish how much time you will spend on each individual trait.

Balancing Values

When you are aware of how much time you are allocating for each value, then you can better balance the values that you teach throughout the semester. This way, it is easier for you to track which values you are teaching your students.

You should in no way think that adding another component to your lesson plans will be time-consuming or create more work. As I suggested earlier, all curricula provide the framework to teach character. As the teacher in the class, all you have to do is highlight the traits that you want students to learn. As you draw more emphasis on each of the traits through measurement, time management, and balance, you will be that much closer to improving character in the classroom.

Building Character behind the Scenes:

As the course progresses and your students are introduced to a balance of core values, they will be more informed about the range of positive values they can choose to take on in order to improve their character.

Francis Rule #13: Create a Classroom that Is Inviting

Character-Building Component: Caring

Students need to be inspired; unfortunately, however, many of our school classrooms include a décor that is anything but inspirational. They lack individuality, colour, and style, as they are all painted in the same off-white shade. When I was lucky enough to get my own room, the look of the classroom was one of the first things that I wanted to change. This change was necessary because developing character is not something that is tied specifically to our lessons; it is also influenced by the environment in which we work and play. With this in mind, I wanted to create a classroom for my students that was inviting, uplifting, and inspirational. So with the approval of my department head and principal, I decided to make some major adjustments. Below are some of the changes that I made that you may find useful should you have the opportunity to decorate your room:

- **Add a touch of paint:** I wanted to paint my room to give it a new look. So I went to the art department and inquired of my colleague if she knew of any students who would be interested in helping. It didn't take long for her to find a couple of eager students. These students would eventually pick my paint colours and oversee the whole project. When they were finished, I was extremely pleased with the results. Adding a splash of colour was one of the best things that I could have done, as it brought vibrancy to the room. The paint went a long way to boosting my and my students' spirits.

- **Hang pictures:** I know that my students look at a lot of pictures every day of various people, especially television personalities and singers. Although I am sure that my students find some of these individuals to be role models, they are not the only inspirational figures I want my students to know. This is why I made a point of purchasing picture frames and putting up pictures of individuals who have made a major contribution to humanity on the walls. I think that we can agree that it is hard to look at individuals like Muhammad Ali, Martin Luther King Jr., or even Michael J. Fox and not feel inspired. These are the types of people I want my students to inquire about. It is good to know that should my students become restless and bored during a lesson, they will have these types of inspirational figures on the walls to keep them company.

- **Quotes:** At the front of my class, directly over my whiteboard, there is an inspirational quote by Winston Churchill that states, "Never, never, never quit." Whenever I receive a new class of students, I explain that these words were uttered by Winston Churchill in World War II during the German air attack on England. When I tell them the story about Adolf Hitler and his attempt to bomb England into submission for some forty-odd days, they always seem quite impressed that Prime Minister Churchill would utter this phrase during an incredible time of peril. It is an important message that I want my students to begin the class with and to remember as our lesson comes to an end. Whether it be on the walls or on class handouts, quotes are a great way to arouse curiosity and get students engaged in conversation.

- **Plants:** Nature has a way of inviting us all to feel inspired. This is why so many of us head to cottages or go for a walk in the park whenever we just want to clear our minds and collect our thoughts. I have made a point of including plants as a part of my décor. I find that it always brings a smile to my students' faces and creates a sense of calmness.

As teachers, it is our responsibility to inspire our students by creating an educational setting that includes strong subject matter and also is aesthetically pleasing. Creating a classroom that is inviting and inspirational is a great way to achieve this goal.

Building Character behind the Scenes:

As students see that you care for your classroom in a way that is creative and orderly, they will begin to care more about you and the classroom you have created.

Francis Rule #14: Remember Birthdays

Character-Building Component: Trust

During my time in university a very special friend of mine managed to always send me a birthday card in the mail. Let me assure you that this was no easy task on her part, because during my university years, I was travelling from city to city to complete my studies. I appreciated her generosity and felt quiet honoured that she took the time to remember my special day. The bottom line is that people in general like to have their birthdays remembered. This little valuable piece of information became especially useful for me once I began teaching. One day, when I was entering grades into the computer, I happened to notice that the marking program displayed the dates of my students' birthdays. As I was looking at the dates, I noticed something very interesting. One of my challenging students and I were born in the same month. In fact, his birthday was just a few days before mine.

As I was entering the grades, I also noticed that this young man had not done well on his last assignment. He was only off by a few points from passing. I could not help feeling bad that I would be handing back a failing grade so close to his birthday. So I decided to do two things. The first was to acknowledge his birthday. I did this by singing my own rendition of "Happy Birthday" (it is very silly and extremely off key), and I also gave the young man a birthday gift of five bonus points that he could use towards any test or assignment. When I handed back the assignment, I took the liberty of incorporating the five bonus points. The young man was thankful for the gift, and he even managed to smile. It was one of the first genuine moments that we shared together. We both still had a long road in regards to improving aspects of his character, but my remembering his birthday definitely allowed us to take a step in that direction. Whether you sing a song, give bonus points, or simply give your student a card, acknowledging birthdays is a great strategy to reveal to your students that you care. This simple act will go a long way to building a bond of trust between you and your students.

Building Character behind the Scenes

Students will begin to believe and trust that you truly have their best interests at heart.

Francis Rule #15: Expect Success (Rather than Failure) from Your Students

Character-Building Component: Perseverance

Towards the end of one particular semester, I remember a conversation I had with a colleague. He was in an uncharacteristically good mood. In particular, he was very happy to be parting ways with two students. Although our conversation was brief, he had much to say about these individuals. You see, he had heard early in the semester from other teachers that these kids had very bad attitudes. I remember him remarking that "this kind of horrible behaviour is exactly what they brought to my class from day one, and not a damn thing changed during our time together." He continued to say, "Thankfully, they are someone else's problem now." I responded to his comments with a comforting smile. However, as I started walking down the hall, I could not help but feel a little taken aback by what he had said. It didn't bother me that he did not want to see these students again, because there probably isn't a teacher anywhere in the world who has not been happy to see certain students leave his or her class at the end of the term. However, what bothered me was that I got the distinct impression that my colleague never really tried to connect with these kids. It seemed like he had made little effort to try to modify any weakness in character that these students may have displayed during the semester. In other words, he expected these students to come in with bad attitudes, and he allowed them to leave with their bad attitudes intact. The question I had after hearing about his disastrous ordeal was: *Could things have been different?*

It is important to remember that when dealing with challenging students, teachers have a large role to play in the ultimate success of these individuals. As a strategy, teachers need to have high expectations for students and then go the extra mile to ensure that these expectations are worked towards. Never expect this task to be easy because more than likely, it will be extremely difficult. Some will argue that you must have both a teacher who is willing to teach and a student who is willing to learn if there is to be any real academic progress made in the classroom. With this point, I most certainly agree. That being said, I do believe that teachers share a large part of the responsibility to make sure this happens. Success in the classroom begins at the top with the mentor and works its way down to the student. The first step is to let students know that you believe that they are capable of success. You will never know what your students are capable of until you are willing to put in the time and effort to find out. If your students are going to have a chance at improving their character and bettering themselves, then you need to reveal from day one that you believe that they can.

I will end this section with the story of an e-mail video attachment sent to me by a vice-principal, who is a friend of mine. On the video was a ten-year-old boy who was the keynote speaker at a teacher's conference in Dallas, Texas. The boy began his presentation by asking the teachers a very heartfelt question. He asked, "Do you believe in me?" He not only asked if the teachers believed in him, but he also asked if they believed in the rest of his classmates. He then said, "You better, because come Monday, we are going to be showing up at your door." It was very moving and inspirational for me to see a ten-year-old boy articulate how important it is to have high expectations for one's students.

Remember, it starts with you. As teachers, we are the front line. We can't afford to pass students' problems on to someone else. We have to put in the effort to try to rebuild weak character even if this brings only minimal returns. We have to believe that each one of our students can succeed at a high level despite his or her past performances. Demand success from your students from the first day, and they will soon understand that this is the standard that has to be met. Let them know that you will not accept any excuses when it comes to improving their characters. You will eventually find that if you set high standards for your students, this will be the standard that they begin to meet and set for themselves.

Building Character behind the Scenes:

If you reveal that you believe in your students, you are teaching them not to give up on themselves.

Francis Rule #16: Provide Up-to-Date Progress Reports

Character-Building Component: Responsibility

In the classroom, there are two sure ways to grab the attention of your students. You can either tell them that they have a pop quiz or you can tell them that you will be handing back their progress reports. I try not to give pop quizzes too often, but when it comes to giving progress reports to my students, I have to say that I am a big fan. As a strategy, I like handing out progress reports regularly because it allows students to confront and take responsibility for what they have or have not achieved. You can give regular progress reports weekly, biweekly, or even at the end of a unit. When you give out reports frequently, it has many benefits for both students and teachers.

For Students:

- Students will be more likely to initiate completing homework and establishing consistent study habits to maintain or improve their marks;

- It reminds students of work that may be outstanding;

- Students can identify if they are meeting classroom expectations. If not, they may want to consider establishing some long and short-term goals;

- It gives students the opportunity to re-evaluate and adjust key elements of their character;

- As students are constantly reminded about where they stand in the class, they can get a sense that their teacher is concerned about their ultimate success.

For Teachers:

- Should students be underachieving, frequent progress reports can remind the teacher of who has fallen behind. This provides plenty of time for steps to be taken to reverse the situation;

- You will be able to stay up-to-date with your marking, as you are constantly handing out updated reports;

- Distributing progress reports creates opportunities for further dialogue. Such dialogue can help to strengthen teacher-student relationships.

Building Character behind the Scenes

Constantly reminding students of their current mark in your class will have them taking your class more seriously. Making them more responsible for their final outcome can improve their overall academic progress in your course.

Francis Rule #17: Try Your Best Not to Send Students to the Office

Character-Building Component: Respect

As an educator, I am sure that you can relate to the fact that, at times, it is very easy to become upset when dealing with challenging students. I remember one day in particular when I was dealing with a challenging student who had been acting in a very disrespectful manner for most of the period. He had not completed any of his work and was distracting other students from completing their's. Despite several warnings to change his behaviour, he continued to act inappropriately. When I asked him (for what seemed like the 'umpteenth' time) to focus and begin his assignment, he told me that I "should stop harassing" him. He then proceeded to say under his breath, "This class is bullsh*t." With that kind of comment, it did not take long for me to feel the tiny hairs on my nearly bald head standing to attention. I was angry and frustrated, and my patience was exhausted. My immediate thought was to send this young man out of my class, as I no longer wanted to deal with him or his attitude. Sending him to the office seemed like the obvious solution. However, knowing this student's troubled past with the administration and other faculty members, I figured that sending him to the office was probably what he was counting on. He knew that he could probably go to the office and give some type of sob story to his vice-principal to justify his behaviour and ultimately receive a minor reprimand. In the process, he would receive exactly what he wanted – the opportunity to avoid completing his classroom work.

Even though I had no desire to have this student in my class any longer, I knew that it was important that he finish his assignment. So I decided in that brief moment to collect my thoughts and I told the young man that he was more than welcome to believe that this class was "bullsh*t," but that did not change the fact that he still needed to graduate. One of the requirements to graduate was to pass this class, and in order pass my class, he would have to finish my assignments, including this one. I then told him to take a few minutes to calm down and then please begin his work. I managed to say these words in a tone that displayed firmness and not the anger that I was feeling. I then proceeded to sit down and began to fumble with some papers on my desk. Truth be told, I did not know what was going to transpire next, and then the unthinkable happened. He muttered a few more words under his breath and then picked up his pen and began his work. The young man's actions definitely caught me off guard. Thankfully, I did not have any more major difficulties with this student for the rest of the period. When the class was over, I asked to speak with him. I let him know that his actions and language were unacceptable. As a result of his actions, he would be writing a two-hundred-word paper outlining why it is important to complete assignments and be respectful. He begrudgingly accepted his consequences and went along to his next class. I learned a lot from this encounter.

As I reflected on this situation, I was pleased with the outcome. Even though every fibre in my body wanted to send this student down to the office, I knew that, in the long run, this would only undermine my influence over him. He needed to respect my classroom rules and authority, not just those of the administration. This is why, as a strategy, sending students to the office should be considered as a last resort. Try to deal with the situation yourself as long as the lines of communication are open and you have not reached an impasse. It is important that you avoid putting on a show in the classroom, so you may want to speak with the student outside of the room and try to resolve the problem there. The bottom line is that your students need to know that you are in charge of your classroom and they need to follow the rules that you have established.

Building Character behind the Scenes:

When students learn to respect your authority, you will find that they will be less likely to commit offences in the classroom.

Francis Rule #18: Lead by Example

Character-Building Component: Citizenship

Most people have a pet peeve of some kind. One of my biggest pet peeves has to do with individuals who litter. I find this type of action speaks poorly of one's character, not to mention the harmful effects it has on the environment. As human beings, we should all take responsibility for our garbage, even when it may be inconvenient to do so. On several occasions, I have even brought garbage home with me because I was unable to find a suitable place to dispose of it during the day. This policy that I have established for myself is one that I expect my students to follow as well. When students come to my class, they quickly come to realize that keeping my classroom clean and organized is a top priority. I make a point to remind my students at the end of each class that they need to pick up any garbage that may be around them. This doesn't always meet with rave reviews, but students know that they will not be going anywhere if they do not comply with this request.

Picking up after oneself is a rule for which I lead by example in my class. If I see garbage on the floor in my classroom, in the halls, or even in the school parking lot, I make sure that I pick it up. Despite having discussed littering for over a paragraph, it is not the focus of this strategy. Rather, I wanted to point out that as teachers, if we want our students to take the policies that we set for them seriously, we need to make every effort to hold ourselves accountable and follow these same policies. Students will be more likely to practice and make routine the policies that we expect of them when we lead by example. I mean, let's face it; it is pretty hard to scold students for breaking rules that we as adults also break or refuse to follow. Unfortunately, on any given day, this occurs in our schools. I remember on one occasion seeing a teacher reprimand a student for wearing his iPod in the hallway. Later on, in that same week, I saw that same teacher wearing an iPod while marking during class. This type of behaviour is hypocritical, and students will easily pick up on this. As a strategy, if you want students to follow the rules of the school and your class, they should not need to look any further than you for a role model. You will find that your students will be able to respect and follow your rules better, and this will allow them to be better citizens in your class and in the community.

Building Character behind the Scenes:

When students see that you practice what you preach, you will have an easier time influencing their character.

Francis Rule #19: Create a "Classroom Rules and Guidelines" Handout

---

Character-Building Component: Responsibility

At the beginning of every new class, there is always a ton of papers to hand out to students, including profile cards, locker information, the course syllabus, and the list seems to go on and on. While these documents are important, there is one document in particular that I could not imagine starting my course without. This document is my "Classroom Rules and Guidelines" handout (CRGH). I consider this document to be essential to building positive relationships with my students, because it lays out the framework of how they should conduct themselves in my classroom. A CRGH can contain the following information about your classroom rules:

- Appropriate dress

- Consequences for cheating

- Policy towards electronic devices

- Policy on eating in class

- Washroom procedures

- Lateness penalties

- Mutual respect

- Suitable language

If you want students to display their best character, they clearly need to know what your expectations are. This is why it is imperative that all of your students receive a copy of your CRGH on the very first day (See Appendix A for a sample copy). Go over this document in class line by line with your students; this way, there is no confusion as to how your class environment is to be maintained. Once your students have been informed of your classroom expectations, have them sign off on the handout with their signature at the bottom of the page. You can even go one step further and have a space where parents can sign as well. This document should go at the front of their binder so that they can see it every time they open it. In the event a student forgets his or her binder, I make sure that I post a copy of the CRGH inside the classroom so there can be no excuses for mis-behavior. Should the rules be broken, it will not be because the students did not know them, but because they were unwilling to follow them. It is at this point that we can have a discussion with students so that they can realize their mistakes and work to correct their behaviour.

Building Character behind the Scenes:

If your students know the rules in advance, there can be little excuse as to why they did not follow them.

Francis Rule #20: Try to Limit the Number of Days You Are Away

Character-Building Component: Responsibility

Taking days off from school is a necessary reality for teachers. Whether it is taking time to look after our families or look after ourselves, there will be days when we will be away from the classroom. However, if you are serious about improving character, you will need to limit the number of days you are away. I say this for the following reasons:

1. Building character requires consistency. Your students need to have a routine that provides consistent structure. If you are not in the classroom, that structure is hard to duplicate by a supply teacher and your students might be inclined to slip back into their old habits.

2. As the teacher in the classroom, you know your students better than anyone else. You know their potential trigger points, and if a student is having an off day, you will be better prepared than anyone else to deal with this situation effectively.

3. Often when supply teachers provide students with work, students tend to regard the material as busy work and not take it seriously. This can lead to a very chaotic period, as students waste time chatting with their friends or playing with their cell phones. Challenging students have a difficult time controlling their behaviour in this environment.

Building character requires a special relationship between the student and the teacher, and this relationship is extremely fragile in the beginning. Any gains you make in improving character during the semester can easily be set back if you are not in the classroom to maintain them. A good example of this was when a colleague of mine took the opportunity to implement a few of the Francis Rules. Regrettably, during the semester, she had to be away on several occasions. When she returned to class, she always noted that the supply teacher had much to comment on: her challenging students had returned to being uncooperative, gone on extended bathroom breaks, and failed to complete assignment after assignment. Many of the kids who had made progress in their character development under my colleague's leadership seemed to slip back into some of their unsavoury habits. My colleague was rightfully upset with the situation. She was upset with the students because she had hoped they would have a done a better job controlling their behaviour. She was hoping that because the students were improving with her, they would have acted appropriately no matter who was in charge of the classroom.

However, with challenging students, this theory does not always translate into reality. This experience taught her a valuable lesson. She realized that these students had a long history of making bad decisions, and they were anything but perfect when it came to exhibiting strong character. These students were easily tempted back into their old habits, and my colleague felt that much of what had happened during her absences could have been avoided had she been in the classroom.

The bottom line is that character development takes time, and it is very hard to build character if the teacher is not there to facilitate this. I am in no way saying that you should not take time off should you need to. I am simply saying that if you can avoid being away from the classroom as you build character with your students, it will certainly help you to achieve this goal.

Building Character behind the Scenes:

As students see that you are committed to them, their character will begin to mature in a direction that is positive and that fosters accountability.

Francis Rule# 21: Role Play

Character-Building Component: All Six Elements of Character

In my classes, I make sure to incorporate as many visual styles of learning as possible. Visual learning aids can include anything from books or magazines, overheads, movies, and of course the internet. As a strategy, one visual aid that I really enjoy using to build character in the classroom is an activity called role play. Role play simply allows students to act out real-life situations in class. It is a great learning tool because it requires that students use a wide variety of skills to complete their presentations. These skills can include memorization, teamwork, leadership, creativity, and improvisation. Students are not just tapping into and learning new skills through role play; they are also learning core values through the vignettes and characters that they become. I really enjoy using role play in my career studies class while teaching the unit on character education. In this unit, my students learn about the six elements of character and then have an opportunity to act out good and bad examples of each of the elements. With a typical high school setting as a place from which to draw examples, these presentations can end up becoming quite amusing.

The students really enjoy acting and watching these performances, as it allows them to identify the kind of character one requires for success and the kind of character that will set one on a path to failure. As this is a visual presentation, the whole class gets the opportunity to learn and discuss these lessons together. For some students, it encourages them to confront some of the negative character traits that they may possess. This activity works well in my careers classes, but this type of activity can work well in any discipline. You could have students observing and analyzing elements of character on a battle scene, during a trial, in a board meeting, or maybe even during a science experiment. Simply put, incorporating role play is a great activity by which students can learn about character. Your students will have fun acting and learning all at the same time.

Building Character behind the Scenes:

By using role play in your classroom students are compelled to recognize those areas of character that are their strengths and confront those areas that leave room for improvement.

Francis Rule# 22: When You Feel Like Quitting and Giving Up on a Student – Don't!

Character-Building Component: Perseverance

There is no doubt that as a teacher, you will meet the kind of challenging student who tests and irritates your very last nerve. I have definitely had my fair share. I remember one student in particular who acted liked he was doing me a favour by coming to class. On the days that he did decide to grace my classroom with his presence, he would come late, without supplies, and would be disruptive throughout the lesson. Despite speaking with his parents, vice-principal, and guidance counsellor about his behaviour, there was little change in his performance. I was becoming increasingly frustrated with this situation. This was in large part because I felt like I was putting in more effort for him to obtain the credit than he was. It reached a point where I became fed up with trying to guide this student to do the right things. If he wanted to fail the course, that was his right, and I no longer would get in his way. In other words, I wanted to give up on him. Does this situation sound familiar?

In the end, I did not quit, and this was due to an old adage I mentioned earlier: "You can lead a horse to water, but you can't force it to drink." This quote described my situation perfectly, as the young man was refusing to drink any of the 'water' that I was offering. However, who is to say that he would not want to have a drink of water at some point? It was then that I realized that I could not just give up on this student. He might not hand in all of my assignments or always be respectful, but as long as he was on my roster and attending my classes, I would use this opportunity to improve his character in some way. This could include working on his tardiness, cutting down on his disruptions in class, or simply helping him refrain from using foul language. The bottom line is that even when faced with adversity, I would not give up on this young man; rather, I would continue to work with him in the hopes of improving just one of his inappropriate practises. In the end he did not pass my course but on our final day together, as I bid him fare well, we did end up shaking hands. It was at this moment that I realized that we were both able to benefit from our time together. It is never too late for our students to want to better themselves. Should we decide to give up on them, both the student and the teacher may never find out the potential of which each is capable.

Building Character behind the Scenes:

Students need to see examples of perseverance in order for them to persevere. If we don't give up on them, there is always the possibility that they might stop their habit of giving up on themselves.

Francis Rule #23: Food for Thought

Character-Building Component: Trustworthiness

Waking up late to go to work usually means that I am in for a chaotic morning. As I am rushing to leave the house, I can forget to do many things, like take out the trash, say good-bye to my family, and leave my lunch in the fridge. On the odd occasion when I do leave my lunch at home, it makes for a very long school day. Trying to lead a lesson on an empty stomach is nothing I look forward to because throughout the entire lesson, all I am thinking about is food. Teaching requires a lot of energy, and without the proper nutrition, it is hard to do the job effectively. I can work around this situation if it occurs once in a while, but I would have a hard time being an effective teacher if this occurred on a regular basis. Unfortunately, going without proper nutrition is a very real scenario for some of our students. Whether it is because they don't have enough time to eat breakfast in the morning or they end up forgetting their lunch (in some cases, some students don't have a lunch to bring), they come to class lacking energy and nutrition, which can affect their overall performance.

It is pretty easy to recognize these students. You may find that they are the ones who are overly hyper, as they snack on candy to fill their stomachs. Or you may just find that these students do not have the energy to listen to lectures and complete assignments because they just feel like sleeping. So as teachers, what can we do? Well, I don't expect you to start buying breakfasts and lunches for your students, but perhaps you could provide them with a small healthy snack. This is why I like to keep healthy snacks, like granola bars, yogurt, or even dried fruit on hand should my students need it. Should you recognize that your students seem a little sluggish, take the time to offer them a small snack. You will find that your students will be very thankful for such a gesture, and it will help to give your students the energy they need to stay engaged during your lesson. It is a small gesture to make, but it is one that can pay off in unimaginable dividends.

Building Character behind the Scenes:

Students will come to appreciate your generosity, and this in turn will create a better bond of respect as they realize that you have their best interests at heart.

Francis Rule# 24: When Giving Assignments, Make Sure that Students Have Received and Understood Your Instructions

Character-Building Component: Trust

Often when we provide instructions for our students to complete in-class assignments, we may assume that all of our students are on the same page and understand what we want them to do; we should not make this assumption. When you ask students if they understand the task that is to be completed, you can rest assured that not everyone understands what is being asked of him or her. Should this individual be one of your challenging students, he or she might be quite hesitant to let you know that the assignment is not clear. Rather than asking for help, these students may stay at their desks and give the impression that they know what they are doing; however, by the time the class is over, they will have completed little or no work at all. If you confront the students and ask them why they did not get their work done, it is only then that they will let you know that they did not understand what was being asked of them. They may assume that not understanding the work is an acceptable excuse for wasting valuable class time, but as teachers, we know that this type of action is unacceptable. A few simple steps will help you to prevent such a scenario from occurring.

The best way to avoid such a situation is to go a little further than asking the students if they understand the assignment. If you suspect that a student does not understand what is being asked of him or her, do not accept a quick "Yes" and nod of the head as confirmation. Simply ask the student to explain your instructions back to you. If he or she can, it will help to clarify things for the student. If he or she cannot, then you need to figure out what it is about your instructions that is causing the student to be confused. If this means going over the assignment line by line to ensure that the student gets it, then this is what needs to be done. However, never make the student feel silly for not understanding what you have written. Anyone can be confused by the simplest of wording, but in the end, it is your responsibility as the teacher to make sure that your students understand the message you are trying to convey. To ensure that students do not feel like they are being singled out, you should ask a few students (of varying abilities) in the room to repeat back the assignment to you. As you continually go out of your way to ensure that your challenging students understand the assignments, you will find a genuine change in their attitudes towards completing their work; you may even find them seeking clarification should they need it. Your students will begin to sense from your efforts that you are sensitive to their needs and are committed to their overall academic progress. Taking this type of initiative will create a classroom environment in which students will be less self-conscious and more empowered to ask for help.

Building Character behind the Scenes:

Students will come to trust that they will not be embarrassed should they need to seek additional clarification.

Francis Rule #25: Make Sure that Students Hold the Door Open for Others When They Enter and Leave Your Classroom

Character-Building Component: Citizenship

If we are going to help our students build character, then we may want to think about reinforcing some basic etiquette skills. I definitely found this needed to occur at my school. As I became acquainted with some of my classes during the first few days of a new semester, I noticed something very surprising. As these students entered my classroom, many of them did not bother to hold the door open for others coming in. In fact, these students moved so quickly through the door that they did not even so much as glance back to see if anyone was coming through it. Call me old-fashioned, but when I was growing up, holding the door open for someone was considered mandatory and not optional in school. I found this type of insensitive behaviour occurring not just in my classroom but also on trips to the library or even on school excursions. It was clear to me that this type of behaviour needed to be addressed.

I immediately brought my concerns to my students, and the discussion was a little awkward at first. The surprised looks on my students' faces made it seem like this was the first time they had heard that holding the door open for someone else was the right thing to do. Some of my students, particularly the males, believed that holding the door open was "uncool." However, I let the students know that I was serious about this policy, and from then on it became a class rule that students must hold the door open for others who are behind them. Despite any initial objections, all of my students quickly got on board. At first, I would have to encourage my students by calling out individual names to hold open the door. If they still resisted, I would go over to the door with the student and we could hold the door open together. However, once students got used to the rule, it became second nature. Now, if we go on a trip inside or outside the school, my students are very mindful of holding the door open for others. You will find that some students will be more eager than others, but the point is to get them in the habit of doing this. You should not attempt to try this strategy if students seem to be in an uncooperative mood, as it can lead to a possible conflict. Only try to implement it if you find the students to be cooperative. The goal here is to eventually have the students take the initiative on their own. As trivial as some may think this action is, holding the door open for someone is extremely important in establishing strong character. It underscores a method of thinking wherein kindness and respect for all people is mandatory to building and maintaining strong character, as well as positive relationships. This type of exercise goes well beyond the classroom, as these skills can be transferred into society. Students will be more inclined to remember to hold the door open, not just for their peers, but for everyday citizens.

Building Character behind the Scenes:

As simple as this act may seem, it will go a long way in helping our students become better citizens in our schools and communities.

Part 3

The Future Shines Bright
Strategies 26 through 50

Francis Rule #26: Timing Is Everything When It Comes to Constructive Criticism

Character-Building Component: Trust

Consider the following scenario: as you are driving to work, you are reminded that soon you will be in the classroom having to interact with one of your least favourite students. You are not looking forward to this encounter because of the constant negativity that arises between the two of you. We know this is how you are feeling as an educator, but have you ever thought about how this student might be feeling as he or she arrives in your class? Perhaps this student is also thinking about the impending confrontation over a missing assignment or a forgotten detention. More than likely, the student is also not looking forward to any negative comments you have about his or her poor performance. This is not a good way for either individual to start the day, so where do we go from here? Clearly, something needs to be done to reduce the tension and frustration that both the teacher and the student are feeling. As the teachers, we are the leaders of the classroom, so we need to make sure that we do our best to minimize potential conflicts. This means that even when students conduct themselves in such a way as to warrant constructive criticism, we must make sure that we provide such criticism at the appropriate time.

Students can be reluctant to come into a classroom if they feel they are going to be constantly bombarded by negativity. There is no doubt that constructive criticism is justified and necessary, but in such cases, teachers should always be mindful of when the comments are taking place. I remember one year when I was dealing with a very challenging student. In the morning when he would arrive late to my class, he and I would get into arguments about his tardiness or failure to complete assignments before he had even made it to his desk. This type of dialogue happened so frequently that this student would start to avoid my class because he knew that I was waiting to reprimand him for being irresponsible in some way. I did not like the way this situation continued to unfold, so I decided to seek some advice from one of my colleagues. Throughout our discussion, my colleague was able to remind me that my job as an educator was not to remind my students constantly of their irresponsibility. Rather, my job as an educator was to improve the individual skills and overall character of my students. This would be hard to do if my students stopped coming to my class or just ignored my comments altogether. Keeping this in mind, I promised myself that things would change the next time we met.

When the student arrived to class on the following day, he was late, just as he had been on many other occasions. Despite my desire to deal with this issue immediately, I simply said, "Good morning," to the student and allowed him to go to his desk and get himself settled. Once the students were all working on their independent work, I asked if I could speak with the young man outside for a minute.

I started off the conversation by telling him how pleased I was that he had made it to class that day despite the fact that he was late (yes, I embellished a little). As I knew that he was a sports fan, we had a small discussion about the final score of a basketball game the night before to break the ice. We then we got to the heart of the matter, which was his outstanding assignments and his tardiness. I asked him if he could come by my office later to get started on one of the assignments that he owed me and told him that the meeting would also serve as his detention for coming to class late.

He agreed, and to my surprise, he actually showed up. He received the assignment and managed to complete the work for class the next day. What he handed in was by no means A-quality work, but with some small revisions, it was enough to put a mark other than zero in my mark book. This experience taught me some valuable lessons. I learned that in dealing with challenging students, timing is everything when it comes to constructive criticism. We need to create dialogue that minimizes embarrassment and personal animosity and keeps the focus on their academic progress. At the end of the day, the goal is to keep our challenging students in our classroom learning and to help steer their academic progress step-by-step in the right direction.

Building Character behind the Scenes:

By not constantly focusing on your students' negative behaviour you can create an opportunity for the lines of communication to stay open between you and your challenging students. As they begin to sense that you recognize and accept that they have both good and bad qualities, you as the teacher will have the opportunity to improve the latter.

Francis Rule #27: Eyes on the Board

Character-Building Component: Responsibility

One of the things I learned in teacher's college was that a student's educational experience should begin the minute he or she enters the room. Over the years, I have that found using a strategy known as a "board assignment" works very well to help achieve this goal. Board assignments consist of various types of probing questions or quotes that are written on the front board for students to see as the first walk into the classroom. As students walk into the classroom, they have a clear view of the board assignment. As they continue to walk towards their seats, the learning for this period has already begun as students are already thinking about the comments that I have written down. This occurs because the question or quote on the front board is directly related to the subject matter that is to be discussed for that period. The effectiviness of this strategy is that it provides an opportunity for students to think about the class subject material before they have even taken their seats. Below is an example of the type of board assignment that could be used in your class:

"There are three types of people in this world: those who make things happen, those who watch things happen and those who wonder what happened." *Mary Kay Ash*

Question for students: What is this board assignment trying to say? Do you agree/ disagree with the author?

The students have three to five minutes to write a response to the question directly below the quote. (I usually ask that my students write at least a paragraph for their response.) After they have finished, we then spend a few minutes discussing the board assignment and begin tying it to the lesson at hand. So I guess you may be wondering how this type of strategy helps to promote strong character. There are three reasons in particular that come to mind:

1. Students often come into a classroom discussing frivolous matters amongst themselves. Teachers then spend a few minutes trying to quell this chatter and get students on track. This can often lead to unwanted student-teacher confrontations. Having an assignment that students must compete immediately as they walk through the door helps to produce a positive routine and minimizes any idle chatter and the chances for unwanted confrontations.

2. Teachers will have a few minutes to take care of beginning-of-class duties (e.g., attendance, profile cards, or collecting assignments) while the students complete the board assignment. This structured system forces students to take responsibility for completing their work immediately as they come through the door.

3. Often some of your challenging students do not want to get involved in class discussions because they feel that they do not know the required answers to the questions that are being asked. Board assignments provide an opportunity for students to get involved without having to necessarily know the right answer. Responses given in class are not necessarily required to have a specific answer; rather, they can be based on one's personal opinion.

Board assignments are an ideal activity for any discipline, whether you are teaching Math, English, History, or Science. You will find that this structured strategy allows all of your students to be more focused and interactive in the lesson. See Appendix B for my Top Ten Inspirational quotes

Building Character behind the Scenes:

When challenging students have too much idle time throughout the class, this can lead to unwanted disruptions. Board assignments help to minimize the idle time in a classroom, which can increase participation and personal responsibility.

Francis Rule #28: Did Someone Say "Field Trip?"

Character-Building Component: Trust

If you have a large group of challenging students in your class, going on a field trip may be the last thing that strikes you as a good idea. However, a field trip may be exactly what is needed to help build genuine relationships with your students. Recently, I went on an excursion with my classes to a local university. I had some apprehensions about taking certain students simply because I did not want to have to be embarrassed by their immature antics. However, after careful consideration, I reconsidered and decided to take the students. I knew that this trip would be informative and useful, as it would open my students' eyes to a variety of career options – so off we went. Thankfully, any fears that I had about "immature antics" were quickly put to rest and what took place was a pleasant experience. Rather than battling students to participate and pay attention, I found that during the trip they were engaged and asked many questions. I was able to bond with several of my challenging students in a way that I had not achieved in the classroom; on this day, (as my students might say) we were just "kicking it." No we were not singing "Kumbaya" together, and there were a few times when I had to remind them to behave themselves; but overall, both the students and I were able to drop our guards, have real conversations with one another, and enjoy the day.

If you want to build genuine relationships with your students, then consider a field trip as a possible step in the right direction. Take the opportunity to point out interesting scenery, discuss life goals, or just sit down and grab a bite together. It could lead to a whole new way of viewing one another. Some teachers may feel that they cannot trust their students to act appropriately while on a field trip and this is a valid concern; at the same time, it is critical that you take the opportunity to show your students that you do trust them. I am not suggesting that you let your students run free without supervision, but allow them to get a sense that, given the opportunity, you believe they will represent their school in a positive light. You will find that if all goes well, all parties involved will have their characters enriched as a result of the experience.

Building Character behind the Scenes

Let students feel like you trust them outside of the class. This can lead to them meeting your expectations and strengthen the trust they have in you to direct them in their education.

Francis Rule #29: Homework Buddies

Character-Building Component: Responsibility

It is no secret that students who are away from the classroom for a day or two can find it difficult to get caught up on missed assignments and classroom work. It can be become quite difficult because these students have to catch up in not just one, but potentially all of their classes. Challenging students who are faced with such a workload can easily become discouraged. They can become frustrated and ultimately give up on completing most of the assignments, if they complete any. To try to offset such a situation, I encourage my students to start completing assignments while they are at home whenever they find that they are going to be absent from school. A good strategy to achieve this goal is to pair your students up with homework buddies at the beginning of the semester.

With the homework buddies strategy, your students will be responsible for getting the names of a few students in the class and exchanging contact information. Students should inform the teacher of the homework buddies they have chosen (ultimately, the teacher will have the final say). I find that using e-mails or texting to contact homework buddies usually works well as a means of communication. Should students find that they are going to be away from class, they can simply get in touch with their homework buddies. This provides students with an opportunity to have a heads-up on the class work they have missed. This way, students can begin completing assignments partially or fully from home. You may find that some of your challenging students are resistant to the idea of having a homework buddy. This type of thinking may be unavoidable, and there is no quick fix for this attitude. Just continue to be persistent and provide your students with as many options as possible for them to be successful. This strategy is a great character-building technique because students are taking a proactive initiative and being responsible for the work they missed as opposed to falling behind and trying to hold their teacher responsible.

Building Character behind the Scenes:

Students can take more responsibility when they are absent to make sure that they complete assignments.

Francis Rule #30: Anywhere but the Back of the Class!

Character-Building Component: Responsibility

On the first day of class, it is quite easy to spot those students who may be challenging to teach throughout the semester. You will find that before you can say, "Good morning" to any of the new recruits, those students who have mischief on their minds make a sharp beeline for the seats at the back of the classroom. One thing I have come to realize throughout my years of teaching is that these seats at the back of the class are considered to be highly valuable to students. They are the equivalent of getting gold seats to the Stanley Cup or getting seats that place you directly on the fifty-yard line for the Super Bowl. They are held to be the best seats in the room because they can provide students with the perfect cover to be secretive and avoid academic responsibilities. It is at the back of the class that students have more of an opportunity to carry on private conversations, use their cell phones for a variety of applications, or just sit and do nothing as the rest of the class unknowingly conceals their covert activities. As the teacher, you should consider these seats to be highly problematic. You should put some serious thought into which students occupy these seats, and if you are going to make seating changes, you should do it sooner rather than later.

With this knowledge in mind, I very much look forward to the first day of class. As students head straight for the back of the classroom, I say absolutely nothing. Once the first student feels that everything thing is okay, they invite more of their like-minded friends to sit beside, in front of, and behind them. I very much appreciate this gesture because in just a few minutes, I am able to identify which students may be setting themselves up for failure. Once this has been confirmed, I quickly reassign these students to new seats. Expect the decision to relocate students to be met with protest. Objections like "I didn't do anything!" and questions like "Why are you asking me to move?" will surely be asked. When this occurs, I simply reply in a very calm tone that "I am not accusing you of doing anything; I am asking you to move because as your teacher, I can." This sends a clear message to your students that you will decide where the best position in the classroom is for them to learn. Your expectations are that all students in the class are to contribute to the classroom environment and not just be a fly on the wall.

Building Character behind the Scenes:

Students want to succeed. As teachers, we must put them in a position that will foster this type of outcome. Putting students in assigned seats will help to create a stronger sense of responsibility and inclusion.

Francis Rule #31: Use a Multitude of Learning Tools to Help Reach Your Students

Character-Building Component: Responsibility

It is quite fair to say that when I first started teaching, I easily made my fair share of mistakes. One mistake that I am about to share with you involved assigning my students three days of book work in a row. On the third day, when I looked out into the class, the zoned-out look on my students' faces said it all – they were bored. Most of my students were able to stay focused and finish the assigned questions; however, my challenging students found it hard to stay engaged. They were whispering back and forth with their friends, trying to text on their cell phones, or just doodling on their desks. Knowing what I know today as an experienced teacher, I realize that three days in a row of textbook work was a huge mistake on my part.

There is nothing wrong with assigning book work, but there is old proverb that I have come to embrace which states that "variety is the spice of life." As educators, it is crucial that we remember that no two students learn exactly the same way. Our classrooms are filled with students who have multiple learning styles, so as a strategy, we have to do our best to make lessons that accommodate these styles. This is particularly crucial when we are teaching those students whom we find challenging. I say this because if you fail to teach from a perspective that creates interest for challenging students, then you may have quite a difficult time keeping them engaged in course work. Below are a handful of basic teaching tools that will help to diversify your lessons and increase student interest:

- **PowerPoint:** This is a great tool for displaying large amounts of information in a manner that is exciting and visually pleasing for students. PowerPoint is a computer software application that allows individuals to display information that would normally be shown via the blackboard or overhead machine. What is interesting is the way in which you present the information. You can incorporate colour pictures, graphs, music, and even videos into your presentation.

- **Internet:** The internet is incredible technology. Use the internet in your classroom to go on a journey anywhere in the world.

- **Guest speakers:** Having guest speakers in the classroom is always a great way to enhance a lesson. Students get to hear from those individuals who are currently in the real world that can provide first hand information about their experiences.

- **Informal discussions:** Students always argue that they never have a chance to be heard, so have guided discussions to give them that voice. This involves no studying or book work and allows to students to offer their opinions on a variety of topics.

- **Newspaper articles:** Students have the opportunity to read about timely stories and respond to recent events in their local communities.

By diversifying your lessons you will see an improvement in the overall character of your students, especially in the area of responsibility, as they will be less likely to get bored and more likely to establish a genuine interest for learning class material.

Building Character behind the Scenes:

Students will feel more connected to the work if it is delivered in a manner that interests and engages them.

Francis Rule #32: No More Excuses

Character-Building Component: Responsibility

Where there is an excuse, you will find that there is never a student too far behind. Excuses amongst high school students are far from the exception and have unfortunately become quite the norm. Students consistently have a variety of reasons for why they cannot succeed at meeting deadlines. "My printer ran out of ink" and "I didn't know that the assignment was due" are some of the most overused excuses I have heard throughout my years of teaching. My response to these types of excuses has always been the same –they are simply unacceptable. I say this because as educators, we are responsible for getting our students ready for the world beyond high school. My experience in the world has taught me that there is little room for excuses.

People want to know what it is you *can* do, not what or why you cannot do something. That being said, I would be doing my students a great disservice if I accepted their invalid or (even valid) excuses on a consistent basis. This may sound harsh to some, but at the end of the day, I do not want my students using excuses as a crutch that they can lean on; if I let them, this is exactly what they would do. When a deadline has been issued for students to hand in an assignment and they fail to do so, they need to be held accountable for their actions. Below are some of the techniques that I use to hold my students accountable:

- **Late marks:** I assign late marks to my students so that they understand that for each day that goes by, their assignment will be worth less and less. (You should consult your board's policy on assessing late marks.)

- **Detentions**: If I find that students are taking too long to hand in their assignments, I may request that they stay after school to get the assignment finished.

- **Final closing date:** For all of my assignments, there is a final closing date. After this date, students will not be permitted to hand in the assignment.

- **Call parents:** Students who seem to have a hard time getting in assignments can expect that I will call home to consult with their parents as to why this is the case and find out what we can do about it.

- **Assign extra work:** If students consistently fail to hand their assignments in on time, they may be asked to complete a second assignment. This assignment is to accompany the first assignment that was handed in late. I usually add a small mark for completing this second assignment.

- **Assign a paper:** Students may have to write a mini-essay outlining why it is important to hand in their assignments on time. This paper can be anywhere from fifty words and up.

These techniques are good ways to help students stay on track and hold them accountable for their actions.

Building Character behind the Scenes

If students know that excuses will not be tolerated in the classroom, they will do a better job of trying to get their work in on time.

Francis Rule #33: Assign Individual Duties to Students

Character-Building Component: All Six Elements of Character

As a teacher, it goes against my intuitive nature to give students who I know are irresponsible, tasks that require a high degree of responsibility. However, despite my uneasiness, I realize that for these students to grow and improve in their character, opportunities for responsibility must be provided to them. A great way to do this is to assign some of my most challenging students duties that require various degrees of responsibility. It is helpful to start off by assigning smaller, in-class duties and then move to duties that have the student leaving the classroom. Below are some of the duties you can assign:

- **Giving handouts to other classmates:** Throughout a lesson, I will ask various students to distribute handouts to their classmates.

- **Take attendance:** A student can be asked at the beginning of class to take attendance. I usually have them call out the names of the students in the class to ensure accuracy.

- **Set up audiovisual equipment:** One or more students can be asked to set up the computer workstation for PowerPoint or internet presentations.

- **Pick up classroom resources from other classes:** Sometimes, I need a resource in the class that I did not anticipate or the office has requested that I pick up a package. When this happens, I will send a student to get these items.

- **Write on the board:** During the class, you can assign a student to write down their classmates verbal responses.

- **Meet guest speakers:** Often, there will be guest speakers who are coming to the class for a presentation. When this occurs, I will send one or two students down to meet them and bring them back to the class.

The above duties can take place inside or outside the classroom. Try not to assign tasks that your students may not be ready for. You are trying to build individual responsibility and the bond of trust between you and the students – this can take time. Remember, you will never know what your students are capable of until you give them a chance.

Building Character behind the Scenes

All six elements of character have the potential to be developed depending upon the task assigned.

Francis Rule #34: Help Encourage Students to Establish Realistic Goals

Character-Building Component: Perseverance

When I was a student in high school, I remember spending a lot of time thinking about nothing really important at all. My thoughts were consumed with socializing, the latest fashion trends, sports, television, and of course dating. I was very much a teenager who was concerned with my life in the present. If you had asked me what I wanted to do in the next five years, I probably would have paused and responded with "I don't know." If you fast-forward to life in the current year, not much has changed with regards to the thoughts that preoccupy the average teenager. Teens today spend huge amounts of time thinking about their life in the here and now. For the most part, there is nothing wrong with living in the moment; however, there needs to be an opportunity for critical thinking about one's future. It is hard to know which direction to go in if you do not know your destination. This is why teens need to take time to think about their future and the steps needed to ensure their success. This is where teachers can play a critical role. Teachers can help students to be successful in the future by providing them with goal-setting strategies in the present. Goal-setting is an excellent activity, because it provides students with a blueprint with the steps necessary to be successful in whichever endeavour they choose. When assigning this task to students, I like to break goals into two separate areas, which consist of short and long-term goals.

Short-term goals can be defined as goals that can be obtained in the near future (e.g., in a day, a week, or even within a few months). Long-term goals can be defined as those goals that one can achieve over a longer period of time (e.g., a semester, a year, or even postgraduation). For each of these two areas, it is useful to have students thinking about their goal setting in terms of both personal and academic goals. Personal goals can include family, spiritual, work, or financial aspects; while academic goals can include education and possible career options. It might be a good idea to have students start off initially establishing one or two goals for both the personal and academic areas. If you find that some of your challenging students are resistant to the idea of goal setting, you may want to have them start thinking about personal goals before they tackle any academic ones. A simple way to have students set this up is to write the following information down on a piece of paper:

My goal:

1. Why is this goal important to me? (Why do I want to pursue this goal?)

2. What is my action plan to achieve this goal? (What steps can I take to make this goal a reality?)

3. Follow up. (Have I kept up with my promises? What have I done since my last entry to make my goal a reality?)

On a piece of paper, leave a few lines between each question. Students can simply repeat the process for any other goals that they want to establish. You should have students check in on their goals weekly or even biweekly, but make sure that you are consistent with this routine. As students begin to monitor their progress, they can take steps to adjust their behaviour to ensure their overall success. If all goes well, by the end of the semester your students can respond with more than just "I don't know" when they are asked about some of their future goals.

Building Character behind the Scenes:

As students begin to accomplish their first goal, the expectation is that they will try to reach another until goal setting becomes a habit.

Francis Rule# 35: Make Sure that Your Students Leave the Classroom as They Found It

Character-Building Component: Citizenship

Before I was fortunate enough to obtain my current permanent teaching position, I was a rookie caught in the unpredictable world of supply teaching. Although I appreciated being a supply teacher, this was something that I did not want to be doing for too long. I enjoyed the opportunity because I gained some great contacts and teaching experience. At the same time, I did not enjoy being in a classroom that was someone else's and not mine. Supplying for someone else can be a challenge for a variety of reasons, but what I found to be particularly difficult was the lack of organization and inspiration that some of these classrooms offered. I would take over classrooms that had paper balls all over the floors, candy wrappers on top of seats and inside the desks, and tables and chairs scattered in no particular fashion. I would see students crumple up paper and just add to the already very chaotic environment. If I were a student who was being asked to come to this type of environment and learn, it would probabaly be the last thing I would want to do. This is why it is necessary to make sure that students are cleaning up after themselves and leaving a clean environment for those students who will use the room in the following period.

As a strategy, teachers should ask their students to pick up garbage, tuck in chairs, and organize desks even if they were not the ones to originally make that mess. This needs to take place at the beginning and end of every class. If students are allowed to have food and drinks inside the classroom, make sure that those items end up in the garbage and not on the floor. You may find this to be hard to implement initially, but once students see that you are committed to this routine, their habits will adjust. They will come to understand that they are leaving a mess for their peers and will begin to second-guess their actions. If we are committed to creating lifelong learners, we have to create an environment that students will want to learn in.

Building Character behind the Scenes:

As students begin to pick up after themselves and others, you will find that this lesson carries well beyond the classroom.

Francis Rule #36: Bring on the Guest Speakers

Character-Building Component: All Six Elements of Character

As teachers, we lecture quite a bit to our students. As a result of speaking as often as we do, students may drown out some of the important messages that we deliver. A good way to keep students continually engaged is to invite guest speakers to come in and share their expertise with your students. As a strategy, guest speakers are a great teaching component to add to any lesson, as these individuals can provide a new sense of energy and excitement. They bring with them real-world experience that students are often interested in hearing. Once a friend (Brian) who played in the CFL (Canadian Football League) came to speak to my students about making it to the CFL and what it takes to be successful in a career. The students loved this presentation. They were literally hanging on to every word as Brian spoke about his life growing up, pursuing his dreams, and dealing with adversity. Brian was able to bring a voice to my class that reminded students that they are indeed in charge of their own futures. This is something that I stress to my students daily, but Brian, as a guest speaker, added a context of reality to which my students were able to relate.

Although I was able to get a professional football player to speak with my students, you do not need a high-profile individual to make a big impact in your classroom. Guest speakers can include parents, business professionals, local athletes, and – my personal favourite – former students. All of these individuals have real-world experience that your students would be interested in hearing about. When you do plan for a guest speaker, book off the entire period as your students will have lots of questions. Before the guest speaker leaves, it is nice to have one of your challenging students present the speaker with a gift; you can use some school paraphernalia for this such as a pen or T-shirt. Enjoy the period. You will not need to prepare and teach a lesson but you will find the class to be highly educational for everyone involved.

Building Character behind the Scenes:

Students will be able to develop different aspects of their character, depending upon the messages your guest speakers deliver.

Francis Rule# 37: Keep in Contact with the Other Teachers of Your Most Challenging Students

Character-Building Component: All Six Elements of Character

As teachers, we can have monotonous routines. We arrive at school to teach, lesson plan, mark, and then go home to repeat the process the following day. This routine can leave little time to see other colleagues from outside our departments. I was reminded of this point recently when I took a break from lesson planning to walk to the office to pick up some materials. Just before I arrived at the office, I met with a colleague whom I had not seen in several weeks. We quickly exchanged pleasantries and began chitchatting about the highs and lows of the semester. When we discovered that we were teaching the same student, she was very interested to know how the student was doing in my class. I informed her that the student had gotten off to a rocky start but as of late was doing very well in the course. My colleague seemed genuinely surprised to hear this information as the student was not making the same progress in her class; she was not handing in assignments and was often coming to class late. My colleague felt like she had hit a brick wall in terms of finding ways to help this student improve her grades.

Knowing that this student was taking the initiative to be responsible in my classroom, I became quite curious to find out how she was doing in her other classes. Both my colleague and I decided to e-mail the other teachers who were teaching this student. We discovered that this particular student was passing three out of the four classes she was taking. We decided that perhaps a meeting with the student would be a good next step to see how we could improve her mark in her fourth class. All four teachers made it very clear to the student that we wanted to see her improve her grades overall. Throughout the rest of the semester, we did a good job of maintaining communication with one another to ensure assignments were being handed in on time. If she did not hand in an assignment in one class, she would get an immediate response from all four of us. The student ended up getting all four credits, and this was due in large part to the collective effort of all four teachers working together. This taught me a valuable lesson. As teachers, we must always remember that we are not alone in our daily battles to educate some of our most challenging students. There are many resources that we can turn to, and one of them is our colleagues. As a strategy, make it a habit to speak with your coworkers and discuss possible strategies to get some of your challenging students back on track. Two heads are always better than one when trying to solve a problem.

Building Character behind the Scenes:

Your students have the ability to grow and develop their characters in many directions when they see that all of their teachers have come to together to help them succeed.

Francis Rule #38: A Little Gift can go a Long Way

Character-Building Component: Caring

Our world today is filled with generous individuals – whether it is Bono, the lead singer from the rock group U2, who works hard to help those who have been afflicted with AIDS, or Al Gore (the former Vice-President of the United States), who tirelessly crusades to protect the environment. These people and others like them have tapped into their generous spirit. They realize that no progress can be made without someone being brave enough to take that first *big* step. In our classrooms, one of the first *big* steps that you can take to help build a healthy relationship with some of your challenging students is to be prepared to offer them a little gift. When I speak of a "little gift," I am in no way suggesting a brand-new car or the latest iPod for your student; rather, I suggest something simple, which could include the following:

- **Pencils, Pens**: Students are notorious for losing their pens and pencils (not to mention those belonging to their teachers). This is why I always keep a few extra of these items in my desk. Just because the student did not bring the appropriate supplies to the class does not mean that his or her learning should come to a halt.

- **Agenda:** If I see that one of my challenging students is having a hard time organizing himself or herself, I can think of no better gift than an agenda. This will help the student to keep track of important dates, assignments, and daily activities.

- **Notebook Dividers:** Your challenging students can begin to feel empowered as they take control and organize their notebooks.

- **Paper:** Where there are students, you will always find someone who needs paper.

- **Bookmarks:** I know that some of your challenging students may not be notorious for their reading, but a bookmark could be the tool to help ignite the desire to read more. Check with your school librarian to see if he or she has any extra ones.

The idea here is to send a clear message that you are interested by investing a little something extra towards the education of your students. You will find that all of these items are fairly inexpensive to purchase (your local Dollar Store can be a great resource for such items). If you are unable to purchase them, perhaps you could go on a little scavenger hunt to visit various departments; once you tell your colleagues what it is you are doing, you will be pleasantly surprised at their generosity. Many of your most challenging students may not be used to receiving random gifts, so such a gesture could go a long way in creating a genuine sense of respect and appreciation.

Building Character behind the Scenes:

When students know that others care about them, they may begin to feel safe and understand that it is okay to show that they care about others too.

Francis Rule #39: To the Best of Your Abilities, Do Not Accept Zeros

Character-Building Component: Responsibility

Zero, zero, zero! As I was running my fingers across my mark book, there seemed to be a very common trend occurring for one of my students. She was failing miserably. As I was noting the multiple zeros beside her name, I could not help but smirk to myself. I had warned her many times that if she did not get her act together, she was not going to pass this course, and that was exactly what happened. I admit that I actually felt pleased that she had gotten her just desserts. I truly believed that seeing such grades would be the best lesson she could learn in the long run. This was my initial reaction, but after some deep reflection, I had to question exactly what that lesson was.

This student learned in my class that should she decide not to hand in her assignments, she would simply receive a mark of zero. It occurred to me that this lesson was one that this student was too familiar with and one that needed to be changed. After having this student in my class, I have made some changes to my teaching style. When students do not hand in assignments, I am resolved that a failing grade is not the appropriate response. Rather, I have made it my policy that in the best interests of the students, they have to complete the assignments that they are so desperately trying to avoid. This does not mean that they have an indefinite time line to hand in assignments, because I do believe in deadlines. However, students can learn more from action than inaction. A student will develop skills, such as understanding and maturity, by confronting the responsibility of completing the assignment, rather than avoiding it altogether. This why I work very hard to follow up on missed assignments. Students in my classes now understand that failure is not an option, and zeros are unacceptable. As I began to set this tone early in my classes, I found that students eventually became more responsible when it came to submitting work on time. My students realized that they might as well hand in assignments on time and receive full marks rather than hand them in late and receive partial credit.

Building Character behind the Scenes:

Students will start to take responsibility for handing in their assignments sooner rather than later.

Francis Rule #40: Students Need to Adapt Their Behaviour to Different Environments

Character-Building Component: Respect

As I was walking down the stairs at school, a group of students were walking by in the hallway chitchatting amongst themselves. They were so absorbed in their conversation that they did not notice me. Now I am not one normally to eavesdrop on student conversations, but because I heard my name being mentioned, my ears perked up. One of the students was explaining to her friends that "Francis' class is serious. His classroom is a completely different environment altogether." She went on to talk about some of the classroom policies as she and her friends disappeared around the corner. That was a good moment for me as it validated some of my teaching practices. These students came to understand that despite their previously established habits, students in my classroom had to adapt their behaviour to the classroom environment, and not the other way around.

For the last several years now, I have been playing a visualisation game for my new students. When they come to my class, I have them close their eyes and visualize themselves leaving their previous classroom. I even have them wave good-bye to their old teacher. The students in the visualization gather their books and head down the hallway towards my classroom. I make sure that I tell them that I am there waiting for them with a smile. I ask them to please take a seat. It is at this point that I ask them to open their eyes and the visualization is over. I immediately tell the students, "Welcome," and that I am happy to have them in my class. I go on to explain that it is important for them to realize that they are entering a completely different environment from the one that they just came from. The rules in their previous class (or the lack thereof) are no longer in effect; they now need to adjust their behaviour to this classroom – my classroom. I let them know that if they can do this, they should have no problem succeeding. If they cannot, perhaps they should see their guidance counsellor and ask if they can change courses.

The reason why I go through this elaborate process is that I want to immediately make it clear for the students that they need to adapt their behaviour to this environment and not the other way around. It concerns me deeply when I see students who are unwilling or unable to recognize that their behaviour needs to change depending upon the environment that they are in. I cannot recall how many times I have seen students behave or speak in inappropriate ways in places like hallways, inside the chapel, or even in front of the school as guests arrive. Their actions can include things like kissing their teeth, burping out loud, and using vulgarity. I have even seen kids changing their clothes in the hallway or passionately making out with their significant other before class starts. It is important that we teach kids that different environments require different behaviours. The way they act at home is different from how they act at church, at school, or even with their friends on the weekend. When kids understand that different environments demand different behaviours, they will be better able to conduct themselves more appropriately.

Building Character behind the Scenes:

Students need to be respectful and modify their behaviours for the different environments that they visit.

Francis Rule #41: Remember, There Is Life beyond High School

Character-Building Component: Citizenship

As an educator and motivational speaker, I have the opportunity to speak to hundreds of students every year. One reality that I try to make very clear to students is that there is life beyond high school. It is not always easy for students to foresee the challenges or responsibilities that await them in life. To make things clearer for them, I like to use a visual time line. Embedded in the following time line is a range of years divided into quarters from years zero to 100. I then draw a big "X" on the timeline between the years zero and 25 and ask the students if they know what the X represents. The students quickly figure out that X represents them. After taking some time to absorb this information, the students quickly begin to see that their years in high school are short compared to their years spent as an adult. However, I point out that these years in high school are critical because what students achieve in their academic careers will have a major impact on their adult lives. This impact can include the type of job they are able to get, their level of income, the neighbourhoods they can live in, and their overall quality of life. Not being responsible during one's high school years can have disastrous results for one's impending future.

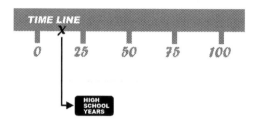

This simple diagram is one that the students have a hard time ignoring. You can see by the looks on their faces their realization that shortly they will move beyond the teenage years into adulthood. You may find a distinct change in some of your students' attitudes as they become more committed to wanting to improve their character. I highly recommend using this time line to get students thinking and talking about their futures sooner rather than later.

Building Character behind the Scenes:

Your students can begin to re-evaluate what they have accomplished to date and what kind of citizen they wish to become.

Francis Rule #42: Play Classical Music

Character-Building Component: Caring

Have you heard the expression that "music can tame the wild beast"? Well, in no way am I referring to students as "beasts" (even though they may at times exhibit similar characteristics), but playing classical music in your classes can help to maintain order in surprising ways. If you have ever heard a good piece of classical music by say, Bach or the Canadian Tenors, then you've probably never forgotten how good this music was for your soul. I first heard about exposing students to classical musical when I was watching an episode of *60 Minutes*. They were running a piece on the tremendous impact classical music was having with students in some of the poorest areas in Venezuela. Some of the most challenging students' lives were transformed when they enrolled in the state-funded classical music program. This program has helped thousands of students and many of them are lower-income, at-risk, and special-needs children. I figured if this program could have the ability to change the direction and overall character of these students, then maybe I should see what classical music could do for the students in my classes.

When I first started playing classical music in my classroom, it was truly priceless to see the looks on some of the students' faces. They didn't know how to react to what they were hearing, and although sometimes some students would protest that they didn't like this type of music, I was truly amazed at the positive impact it had in my classroom. As I played the music in the background during a lesson or as my students worked independently, I found the classroom environment would take on an air of calmness. Students (even my most challenging ones) would become introspective and more engaged in their work. As I marked their assignments, I noticed that the quality of work they were handing in had improved greatly. Students were taking the time to be more insightful and starting to care about the type of work they were submitting. In fact, they would even request that I put in a classical CD on days that I might forget. I found that playing classical music provided the musical distraction that my students craved but also stimulated their minds in a positive way. The bottom line is that you never know how your students will react to new things until you try them, and in my classes classical music worked. It helped me to open my students up to trying new things and to manage my classroom, and it has only had a positive impact on their characters.

Building Character behind the Scenes:

Music has the power to evoke passion. As students become more introspective, they will begin to care more about academics and less about wasting time.

Francis Rule #43: Maintain a Classroom Environment Where Students Show Respect for Adults and Other Students

Character-Building Component: Respect

Although all school boards incorporate respect as part of their value set, it is largely left up to the teachers to make sure that respect is present in their classrooms. We know that students need to respect the adults of the school, but students must also respect one another. In a classroom, this must occur in two key areas: when listening to the opinions of others and when interacting with people of a cultural background that differs from one's own.

Listening to the Opinions of Others

It is not always easy to listen to the opinions of others, particularly if you do not agree with them. In no way do students have to agree with all or any of the comments and opinions that their classmates share, but they do need to be respectful and let other students finish their thoughts. I have seen too many cases where students are trying to get their point of view across in a discussion and before they are done, they are interrupted by a student who suggests they are "wrong" or that their comments are "stupid." As classroom facilitators, we need to create an environment in which students feel free to voice their opinions. Once the student has made his or her comments, have other students wait a few minutes to digest what has been said and then respond. This helps to promote genuine and respectful discussions in the classrooms.

Nigel Francis

Respect for Other Cultures

High schools are places where students interact with a variety of races and cultures that are different from their own. It is without question that as educators, we need to create classroom environments that acknowledge and respect these differences. Oftentimes, students may make jokes in your classes that they interpret as being innocent. However, when students start to make remarks about other races or cultures, there will always be a student in your classroom who is not impressed with these comments and may take offence. I have learned the hard way that a cultural joke that some may view as lighthearted and innocent can be viewed as quite harsh to someone else.

A good example of this was when a few of my students were having a silly conversation with each other about one particular cultural group. Before I knew it, a person made a joking comment that got a few laughs. This led to another comment and another until the entire class erupted in laughter. One young lady who was of this culture suddenly became very quiet. She did not say another word for the rest of the class. She soon asked if she could leave the class to go to the washroom. I learned afterwards that the young lady had been crying in the bathroom because of the comments that were made. I learned a valuable lesson on this day. I don't want students to ridicule their classmates because of their race or cultural beliefs even if the person making the comments is of that culture. I do believe that there is a time and a place where we can make fun of those things that make us different from one another, but I am not convinced that the classroom is the place where this should happen. Creating classrooms where students and teachers are respected must be a top priority for teachers.

Building Character behind the Scenes:

When students respect one another in the classroom, the respect they practice can carry over into their daily lives.

Francis Rule #44: Build Character through Self-Reflection and Analysis

Character-Building Component: All Six Elements of Character

In the classroom, students are used to hearing constructive criticism, but that does not mean that they always want to hear what their teachers have to say. In fact, as stated earlier in this book, if students hear too much criticism from their teachers, they may be inclined to tune out or ignore these comments. That being said, it is important that students learn about the mistakes they may be making. This is why it can be helpful for students to learn about their mistakes not just from their teachers but also from their peers. As a teacher, I have come to learn that teens listen to teens. This is why in my classes I like to provide a series of peer-reflection assignments that allow students to analyze adolescent behaviour. One assignment I use is to have students read the following scenario (or something similar) and then answer the question that follows. The scenario goes like this:

> Terrence is an adolescent whose parents have recently divorced. He now lives with his mother and sees his father periodically. To make ends meet, his mom works six days a week and her work schedule often fluctuates. This means that some evenings, Terrence has to care for himself, but his mother is always mindful to make Terrence dinner if she will not be home in the evening. At school, Terrence is not doing well. His grades are low; he is constantly skipping classes, rarely does his homework, and at times, can be quite rude to his teachers. He knows his mom does

not approve of this behaviour, but he seems to be having
a hard time motivating himself to do better.

At the bottom of story, I ask the class a simple question: "Based
on what you read, is Terrence acting responsibly? Explain why or
why not." I am always very interested to hear the responses of my
students after reading this story. Some students say that Terrence
is acting responsibly. They point out that at least Terrence is going
to school and getting his credits even if he has low marks. Some
students answer that Terrence is not acting responsibly but that we
should not be too quick to judge him. He is probably having a hard
time dealing with his parents' divorce. They feel that perhaps he
has too much responsibility at his age. It sounds like he has had a
hard time since his parents divorced as he spends most of his time
with his mom and takes care of himself on many nights. Perhaps
we should, in fact, give him a break. While there are those who
defend Terrence, other students are quick to point out his flaws.
They suggest that despite the fact that Terrence has had some
difficulties, his current actions are not making the situation better
but worse. They say that his mom has enough problems dealing
with her divorce and taking care of the bills. They point out that
despite her difficulties, she has managed to keep it together and
so should he.

These are all valid responses that provide an interesting dialogue.
However, what I like most about these types of assignments is that
it is the students themselves who are leading the discussion and
pointing out the pros and cons. They learn from their dialogue
about what is right and what is wrong. As the teacher, I try not to
take sides; my role is simply to facilitate. Whether it is through a
story or a writing activity, it is important to have students analyze
the type of individual that they are and the type of person that

they want to become. Peer-oriented assessments are a great way to achieve that goal.

Building Character behind the Scenes:

The character benefit will change for this rule depending upon the assignment you provide. In the case of the scenario previously mentioned, responsibility would have been a key character building component.

Francis Rule# 45: No Sleeping

Character-Building Component: Citizenship

Have you ever walked by a classroom and observed a lesson going on with students sleeping at their desks? To their credit, students can be quite creative by making pillows out of knapsacks or pretending to read their work with their books in their lap and their heads on the desk. However, this is never in the students' best interests. It goes without saying that students come to school to learn, and it is hard to do that when they decide to take a little morning or afternoon siesta in the class. If they are tired, this more than likely means that they did not get a good night's sleep the night before. I have heard my students tell me that they have gone to bed as late 3:00 in the morning after occupying their time with social media sites or downloading music. Students should clearly not be going to bed this late; the classroom cannot be a place where they can get caught up on their sleep. Students need to make better decisions about how they use their time in the evening, and they need to know that if they are making bad choices they cannot make additional ones by sleeping in your class. Should you find that your students are a little on the tired side, below are some strategies to help your students stay awake:

- **Prepare good lessons:** If the class is fun and interactive it will be hard for the students to a fall asleep.

- **Leave the classroom to stretch or get a drink of water:** If you notice that students are nodding off, allow them a few minutes to leave the classroom to stretch or get a drink of water.

- **Have students sit in the front row:** If students are sleeping at the back of the class, try to move them to the front where they can be more engaged.

- **Lights on:** Never turn the lights completely off in your class when using overheads or videos. This gives students the perfect opportunity to sleep.

- **Group work:** Have the students work in groups to allow them to be active. Students might avoid trying to sleep if they know that they need to contribute to a group assignment.

If students have a legitimate reason as to why their head might be down (e.g., they have a headache or they feel sick), then by all means, they should rest. However, this should take place at the nurse's office, not in class. As you set the tone that your classroom is a place where students must come to be engaged, they will have no choice but to accommodate this request.

Building Character behind the Scenes:

Students will learn how to conduct themselves in the classroom community.

Francis Rule #46: Document Misbehaviours

Character-Building Component: Responsibility

When dealing with challenging students, it is in your best interest to record any incidents of inappropriate behaviour. A great tool to help you do this is a document known as a profile card. If a profile card sounds familiar to you, it should. In most schools, they are provided to teachers at the beginning of each semester. Profile cards allow teachers to collect important data, such as students' home addresses and their parent/guardian contact information. Additionally, they provide a space to record student misbehaviours – this is quite important. When documenting student misbehaviour, incidents should be recorded accurately and consistently, as this information will ultimately help to improve the behaviour and the character of the student. Below are some reasons why I suggest using this tool.

It's a Visual for Students

Having worked with challenging students, one thing that I have come to learn is that students never seem to think that their behaviour is a quite as bad as the teacher makes it out to be. This was definitely the case with a student who was coming to class late a little too frequently. When I confronted her, she told me to "chill out" because this was only her second time being late, and there was no need for me to harass her like this. I perceived her response as over the top, but I kept my composure and told the student that I did not realize that inquiring about why she was late was now considered harassment. However, if she felt like she was being harassed, she could go down to the principal's office to report the incident during her lunch. That being said, I allowed her to view her profile card and informed her that she was mistaken, as this was the fourth time that she had been late to class. She looked surprised and even tried to suggest that the dates were incorrect, but I informed her that the dates on the profile card were accurate and that she would have to serve a detention after school as a result. With the evidence in hand, there was not much she could do but take responsibility for her actions. Keeping such records up-to-date so students can see their track record forces them to confront their reality. The goal then is to have students re-evaluate their actions and improve their behaviour overall.

It's a Visual for Parents

Just as profile cards can force students to confront their realities, they can also help to paint a clear picture for parents as to how their children are conducting themselves during the day. Such has been the case on a variety of occasions when I met with parents. I recall one time when a parent had learned about an incident that had occurred at school and had only heard the child's side of the story. The parent came in with the child to hear my side of things. It was at this point that I pulled out the student's profile card and listed the events as they happened. The parent quickly learned of some major details that the student had left out. With the facts on paper, the parent was able to speak to the son about what he had done wrong in the situation. This allowed us to get to a point where we could discuss how we could avoid this type of behaviour in the future.

It's a Visual for Teachers

You probably know that a semester can seem like an eternity when dealing with challenging students. This is because during that time, a variety of misbehaviours can take place in the classroom. Recording moments of misbehaviour on a student profile card can benefit both parents and students, but it can also help teachers have a clear view of a student's behavioural history. Such an analysis provides an opportunity to view the disruptions that have occurred and the steps taken by the teacher to remedy the situation. As teachers, we do not want to find ourselves in situations in which we are using the same strategy to deal with behavioural issues if the strategy is not working. This is why documentation provides the perfect opportunity to identify those strategies that work and those that do not and then make the necessary changes to try to improve our disciplinary actions.

As was mentioned earlier, documenting behaviour can allow parents, students, and teachers to view events accurately as they occurred. This will ultimately provide the necessary insight to help students improve their behaviour and character.

Building Character behind the Scenes:

When you confront students with disruptive behaviour that has been documented, you can challenge them to be more accountable and responsible for themselves.

Francis Rule #47: E-mail Anyone!

Character-Building Component: Responsibility

Each semester brings with it a set of unique challenges when dealing with challenging students. One of those can be trying to reach the parents of a student who is misbehaving in your class. This was the case for me with a student who came to my classroom with a rocky past of tardiness and failing to complete assignments. His behaviour changed drastically in part because of a little invention known as e-mail. In Francis Rule #8, I stated that it is important that we speak with parents as often as we can regarding the progress of their children. Knowing this student's past and the fact that previous teachers had had a hard time getting in contact with his parents, I decided to make a call home during the honeymoon phase of the semester (the first two weeks of school). I was not calling home because the young man had done anything wrong; I just wanted to introduce myself to the parents as their son's teacher and find out what was the best number I could use to reach them. I was lucky enough to catch Dad at home. He was a truck driver and was constantly on the road. His wife did not speak any English and rarely answered the phone. He was happy to hear from me because with his profession, he rarely got to talk with any of his son's teachers.

He suggested that the best way to contact him was by e-mail, as he checked his e-mail regularly while he was on the road. I did as he requested, but I proceeded with caution. I never sent overly wordy e-mails to the parent, and I always sent them during school hours. I would state my concerns (e.g., his son had failed to hand in a certain assignment or had missed a class) and asked if he could get in contact with me to discuss the matter further. I always printed a copy of the e-mail and attached it to the student's file so that the administration would be aware of the nature of the e-mails. This system worked very well, as I always had a response from Dad within 24 hours. Once the young man figured out that he could not hide his indiscretions from his parents, his behaviour and marks improved. Using e-mail as a way of communicating with parents who may be hard to reach using traditional methods can be helpful in keeping them informed about their child's progress.

Building Character behind the Scenes:

When students know that you are just a click away from communicating with their parents, they will be more inclined to act in a responsible manner during class.

Francis Rule #48: Get to Know Your Students outside of the Classroom

Character-Building Component: Trustworthiness

If you were to visit me during the lunch hour, there is a good chance that you would find me eating with the students in the cafeteria. This may seem a little odd to you, as it did for me when I first experienced my teacher supervisor (in teacher's college) doing the same thing. Every day, he brought a packed lunch, including a drink box, and sat down with the students for a little chow time. The one thing that I noticed almost immediately was his change in attitude from his classroom demeanour. This was a teacher who had a good professional relationship with his students, but outside of the class, I noticed a more playful and easygoing side to him. There were no attitudes or reprimands, just a few laughs over the silliest of topics. At first, I thought maybe he just had extended-duty, but this turned out not to be the case. He eventually let me know that to try to help all of his students succeed, he needed first to build a genuine relationship with them. This is not easy to do if your only interaction with your students is inside the classroom. Interaction needs to occur outside of the class where students and teachers can put the pens and papers down, relax, and hang out. I am not suggesting that you chat with your students on social-networking sites, as this should be avoided. However, during the school day, take the opportunity to discuss something other than academics in a casual setting.

I strongly admired his approach to teaching, and this is why I have blended his style with my own. I make a point to eat with my students a few times a month. During this time, I can end up having some of the most entertaining conversations with some of my most challenging students. We can discuss the latest sports scores, electronic devices, extracurricular activities, or even the latest school gossip (yes, I said school gossip). As I hear students talk about issues that are important to them, it provides me with an opportunity to offer some advice. Thus, I am still continuing to educate my students and helping them to develop their characters without having to necessarily wear my formal teacher cap. If you find that eating lunch with your students is not exactly your style, then just take an opportunity to walk through the cafeteria once in a while and strike up a conversation. You can even move beyond the cafeteria and join school clubs such as student council or other extra curricular activities, on a full-time or part-time basis. If not this, then just go out to a school sporting event to cheer students on and let them see your school spirit.

Building a repertoire with students outside of the class is extremely helpful if your goal is to help improve their character. It allows your students to relate to you as more than just an authoritative figure, and you get to view them as more than just challenging individuals.

Building Character behind the Scenes:

Students will come to trust you and your interests in them if they feel you are concerned with their interests outside of the classroom.

Francis Rule #49: The More Visible and Engaged You Are in the Class, the Better

Character Building Component: Responsibility

As the teacher in the classroom, it is important that you make your presence felt, especially when the students are doing group work. Group work is a great way to have students learn a variety of skills, such as teamwork and leadership, but it is also an opportunity for students to become distracted. Without proper supervision, students will often check or write messages on their cell phones, listen to their iPods, or just work on assignments that are due for other classes. A way to prevent such behaviour is to make sure that you are also getting involved in the assignments. This can be accomplished by doing the following:

- **Check in on the groups:** When you assign group work, do not just return to your desk assuming that your students are following through with their assigned duties. Walk around the classroom checking in on the groups regularly; you can help them to brainstorm and listen to their ideas. You want students to feel that the work they are doing is important, so make sure that you engage in the assignment to the same degree as you expect from the students.

- **Set time limits:** Every time you provide group work, you should allocate specific amounts of time for each of the various parts of the assignment. My rule of thumb is to assign less, not more time. Once the time has expired, check in with the groups to see where they are at. If you see that they genuinely need more time, then provide it. You will find that students will be more inclined to stay on task and complete the assignment if there are clear time lines presented.

- **Ask questions:** Make sure that you are asking questions of the group members, especially those whom you find challenging to teach. These questions can be as structured as, "What work have you completed thus far?" or as informal as, "How is your research going?" Whatever question you ask, you want students to get a sense that their opinions and contributions matter.

In each class, we should be as involved as our students, learning and engaging in the subject matter. Students to need to practice being efficient in group settings, and we should never assume that this is a skill that they have mastered. Provide an environment that supports responsibility, and show students that you care about their work.

Building Character behind the Scenes:

Students will become more responsible for completing class work if you reveal to them (through your own engagement) that this work is important to you.

Francis Rule #50: Remember, at the End of the Day, These Individuals Are Just Kids

Character-Building Component: Trust

In a previous year, on the last day of school, as students came to pick up their report cards, I could not help but notice their demeanours. All of them had smiles on their faces. Many of them dressed in shorts and casual tops. As they waited in line to receive their final grades, some had iPods on, while others were discussing their summer plans. All the students seemed to be soaking up the sunshine, and they were ready to embrace the adventures that came with summer vacation. There were tons of well wishes being exchanged back and forth, and there was no tension between the staff and any of the students. It struck me at this time that some of the students whom I and other staff members perceived as negative and challenging to teach were in fact capable of smiling, interacting, and listening. Some of these same students whom I had witnessed fighting, swearing, and being habitually truant were acting in a completely responsible manner. On this day, they were just your everyday kids. They enjoyed listening to music, dreaming about their future summer plans, and laughing with others.

I know that when you have been having difficulties with challenging students, it can be hard to see them as anything other than difficult. However, as teachers we must try to move past that and accept the fact that our students have many sides to their personalities. It is unfortunate that more often than not, you may see parts of their personalities that are unpleasant, but realize that these individuals are not entirely negative. It is helpful to remember that all of us were once students who made mistakes; and we should refrain from demonizing adolescents whose behaviours we too may have tried on for size in days past. Rather, we should strive to be the guiding post (or mentors) that we would have liked to have (or did have) when we were navigating our teenage years. If we are honest with ourselves, we should realize that young people will always try to get away with as much as they can. As a teacher, if you can understand and accept this, then you will find that you will have less ambivilance towards these students. Always remember that you are the adult in the room; you have life experience that extends far beyond that of your students. Your students are simply trying to make it up as they go along.

Building Character behind the Scenes:

Although students may act like and think they are adults, they actually crave leadership and guidance that they can trust. As you provide this, they will begin to defer to your experience and wisdom.

Afterword

There is no question that, as Booker T. Washington once said, "Character is power." As educators, we need to help all of our students embody this ideology. Respect, Responsibility, Perseverance, Caring, Citizenship, and Trustworthiness, are all elements of character that our students need to develop to ultimately achieve their life goals. It will not be an easy task to accomplish when dealing with challenging students, but because you have taken the time to seek out additional resources, I am confident that you have the skill set to work through this challenge. In Part 1 of this book, entitled "Dreams Versus Reality," it was my intention to take you on a journey to remind you of what you already know: that with determination and conviction there is no obstacle you cannot overcome. This school year, expect to have students who are far from ideal. They will come to your class acting irresponsibly, lacking in organizational skills, and at times even being confrontational and argumentative. It is in these moments that you will be challenged most as an educator. Remember, these are not bad students, nor as Michael Josephson states, "… is their character permanently fixed." These students want success, but they have misguided values. As educators, it is our job to reshape those values.

To help you work through some of these challenges and strengthen your students' characters, I provided a variety of strategies in Part 2 ("A New Beginning") and Part 3 ("The Future Shines Bright").

Some of the key strategies that I want to remind you of are the following:

1. Make sure that you are consistently communicating with parents. They need to know how their child is performing and any concerns that you have should be relayed to them in a timely manner to help improve their child's behaviour.

2. In times of conflict, do not take any of your students' inappropriate actions personally. As you want your challenging students to take their academics seriously and they do not wish to comply, there are bound to be acts of defiance. This defiance has much to do with their inadequacies and little to do with you and your classroom rules.

3. Get to know your students outside of the classroom. Take the opportunity to speak with challenging students about topics beyond academics. The bottom line is to build a relationship during the school day that extends beyond the classroom.

4. Finally, be real about your expectations, as your students are not going to change their characters overnight.

As teachers, we have been given a mandate to help all of our young citizens grow and realize their potentials. The strategies outlined in this book will help you, in part, to do just that. Thank you for taking the time to seek out new ways to develop character in your classrooms. It is obvious that you want the best for your students, and I wish you much success this school year. Have fun teaching and use the confidence you have gained through this text to do the unthinkable by *Teaching the Unteachable Student*.

Bibliography

Cherniss, Hilary, and Sara Jane Sluke. *The Complete Idiot's Guide to Surviving Peer Peer Pressure for Teens.* New York: Alpha Books, 2001.

Josephson, Michael S., ed. *The Power of Character.* 2nd ed. Bloomington, Indiana: Unlimited Publishing, 1998.

Scanio, Donna J. *Character Education in the Classroom: Student Handbook.* Bloomington, Indiana: AuthorHouse, 2005.

Appendix A

Francis' Seven Classroom Commandments

Welcome! My name is Mr. Francis and I'm very excited to have you as a new member of this class. As a new student, it is very important that you understand and comply with the following seven classroom commandments:

1. RESPECT: This class will be based on this sole principle.

Respect yourself, others, and your surroundings. We may not always agree, but we must learn to respect the opinions of others.

2. READINESS: Come to class prepared and in full uniform.

Arrive on time and with your agenda, a binder with paper, dividers, pens, and your textbook. Please do not bring your **PEDS** (Personal Electronic Devices) to class. If you are found in possession of these devices, you will be asked to place them on my desk and they will be returned to you at the end of the class. If this becomes a regular occurrence, a variety of disciplinary actions will take place.

3. WASHROOM BREAKS:

Washroom breaks will be permitted; however, only one student can leave the class at a time. Please go to the bathroom and return promptly to class. If the teacher determines that a student is abusing this policy, a variety of disciplinary actions will take place which may include a loss of bathroom privileges.

4. CLEANLINESS: Let's leave the classroom in better shape than we found it.

Before class is over, please clean up after yourselves, straighten out your desk, and tuck in your chair.

5. PUNCTUALITY: Be on time.

Be on time for class – all students should be in their seats once the bell rings. Students who are consistently late will face a variety of disciplinary actions.

6. NO JUNK FOOD IN CLASS:

Students may bring healthy snacks such as fruit, granola bars, or water to class. However, there is absolutely no junk food of any kind allowed. Your consumption of healthy food items should not disturb others around you. Your teacher will have the final say as to what is considered to be an appropriate snack.

7. NO SWEARING:

Students should refrain from using inappropriate language in the classroom. Simply put, if you can't say it in church, then you should not be saying it in here.

Following these seven commandments will ensure our time together will be productive and enjoyable.

I understand these seven commandments and agree to abide by them in the classroom.

Student Signature: _____

Date: _____

Appendix B

Francis' Top Ten Inspirational Quotes

1. "I have a dream…[that children] will one day live in a Nation where they will not be judged by the color of their skin but by the content of their character."

   Martin Luther King Jr.

2. "My friends, love is better than anger. Hope is better than fear. Optimism is better than despair. So let us be loving, hopeful and optimistic. And we'll change the world."

   Jack Layton

3. "A [person] is but a product of [their] thoughts, what [they] think [they] become."

   Mahatma Ghandi

4. "History, despite its wrenching pain, cannot be unlived, but if faced with courage, need not be faced again"

   Maya Angelou

5. "Change will not come if we wait for some other person or some other time. We are the ones that we

have been waiting for; we are the change that we seek."

Barack Obama

6. "Through violence, you may 'solve' one problem, but you sow the seeds for another"

Dalai Lama

7. "I learned that courage was not the absence of fear, but the triumph over it. The brave [person] is not [one] who does not feel afraid, but [one] who conquers that fear."

Nelson Mandela

8. "If you look at what you have in life, you'll always have more. If you look at what you don't have in life, you'll never have enough."

Oprah Winfrey

9. "I am careful not to confuse excellence with perfection. Excellence I can reach for; perfection is God's business."

Michael J. Fox

10. "I've failed over and over and over again in my life and that is why I succeed."

Michael Jordan